WHATEVER IT TAKES

Ruthless Power and Suffering Genius

Peter Deakin

HALSTEAD PRESS

CANBERRA MMXVIII
Published by Halstead Press
Gorman House, Ainslie Avenue
Braddon, Australian Capital Territory, 2612

and

Unit 66, 89 Jones Street
Ultimo, New South Wales, 2007

Typeset by Mark Rashleigh. Printed in Australia by Ligare.

ISBN: 9781925043433

Contents

Preface	5
PART ONE Ruthless Power	7
Niccolo Machiavelli	15
Julius Caesar	22
Emperor Justinian I	28
Emperor Charlemagne	35
Pope Innocent III	39
King Henry V	43
Sir Thomas More	48
Tsar Peter the Great	54
Oliver Cromwell	58
Napoleon Bonaparte	63
Admiral Horatio Nelson	69
Themistocles	75
The Salem Witch Trials	81
Abraham Lincoln	86
Ranavalona, Queen of Madagascar	95
Aung San Suu Kyi	102
Conclusion	109
PART TWO Suffering Genius	113
The Altamira Cave Paintings	120
Michelangelo	124
John Milton	131
Ludwig van Beethoven	135
George Gordon Lord Byron	142
Franz Schubert	147
Robert Schumann	151
Charles Baudelaire	155
Pyotr Tchaikovsky	161
Paul Gauguin	167
Vincent van Gogh	171
Henri de Toulouse-Lautrec	177
Virginia Woolf	181
Ernest Hemingway	186
Charles Bukowski	195
Conclusion	200
Further Reading	203
Index of Names	207

Illustrations

Niccolo Machiavelli by Santi di Tito, 16th Century 16
Julius Caesar by Clara Grosch, 1892 24
Justinian I, Contemporary mosaic, Basilica of San Vitale, Ravenna 29
Charlemagne by Albrecht Dürer, 1511–13 36
Innocent III, Fresco, Sacro Speco, Subiaco, c1219 40
Henry V by Benjamin Burnell 45
Thomas More by Hans Holbein, 1527 49
Peter the Great by Paul Delaroche, 1838 56
Oliver Cromwell, Statue, St Ives, Cambridgeshire, 1901 60
Horatio Nelson by Lemuel Francis Abbott, 1797 71
Themistocles, Engraving by Evald Hansen, 1875 76
Abraham Lincoln by Anthony Berger, 1864 87
The Wrestlers, Roman marble copy after a Greek original 113
Michelangelo by Daniele da Volterra, c1544 125
John Milton by unknown, c1629 132
Ludwig van Beethoven by Joseph Karl Stieler, 1820 136
Lord Byron by Thomas Phillips, 1813 144
Franz Schubert by Josef Kriehuber, 1846 148
Robert Schumann by Josef Kriehuber, 1839 152
Charles Baudelaire by Etienne Carjat, c1863 156
Paul Gauguin, Self portrait, 1885 168
Vincent van Gogh, Self portrait, 1889 172
Henri de Toulouse-Lautrec by Paul Sescau, 1894 178
Virginia Woolf by unknown, 1927 182
Ernest Hemingway by Yousuf Karsh, 1957 187

Preface

WHAT DO JULIUS CAESAR, Pope Innocent III, Thomas More, Napoleon and Lincoln all have in common? What enabled a blind Milton, a deaf Beethoven, a syphilitic Schubert and a certifiable Virginia Woolf and van Gogh to create their memorable masterpieces?

The answer is that each of them, along with all the other characters we will encounter, was able to summon *Whatever it Takes* to surmount any opposition or obstacles lying in their path, in order to leave an indelible mark on the world. In military, political and artistic fields, they found strengths that perhaps we all possess to some degree, to achieve their ambitions.

My examples are some of the best and some of the worst of humanity—the worst, for the purposes of this book, are not the evil barbarians, tyrants and dictators who have inflicted so much death and misery on the world, but rather more interesting figures from history, who were inherently good, or at least well intentioned, yet felt compelled to resort to actions we would regard as at least immoral to achieve their goals. The best are examples of artists, composers and writers who overcame extreme adversity to produce sublime and inspiring work.

Those of the first group were ruthlessly ambitious leaders who were prepared to employ and even abuse whatever power they were able to acquire to further their aims, no matter what misery or suffering they inflicted. The second group are the creative geniuses who suffered far greater pain and misery than they ever inflicted on others, seemingly as the price they had to pay to be able to conjure up their unique masterpieces.

Each group can be seen as the flip side of the same human coin, united by a determination to overcome whatever stood in their way to fulfil their very different ambitions. They all managed to apply *Whatever it Takes* to master what fate threw at them.

The first part of this book deals with the worst—drawing from history a summary of the lives and actions of people who were inspirational leaders, but who were prepared to use whatever methods were necessary to fulfil what they saw as their destiny. Their approach may have been questionable, in many cases cruel, but they believed the end justified their means of achieving it.

The second part will hopefully restore faith in humanity, by tracing works of genius produced out of desperate and frequently tragic situations. It examines the creative lives of artists, composers and writers, who were somehow able to overcome the adversity of their condition, to produce some of the most superb paintings, music and literature the world has known.

Part One

Ruthless Power

Introduction

OUR PLANET IS LITTERED WITH MILLIONS OF CORPSES slaughtered in conflicts waged by ambitious and ruthless individuals. In the 20th century alone, up until 1987, according to meticulous research and data analysis conducted by Professor R.J. Rummel, there were 38,500,000 battle dead—but the figure for civilians killed in armed conflicts was more than four times that: 151 million.

Rummel's central message is that what he calls "democide", namely murder by governments, occurs to a far greater extent under totalitarian regimes, and is significantly less prevalent under democracies:

> The less freedom people have, the greater the violence; the more freedom, the less the violence . . . The problem is Power. The solution is democracy. The course of action is to foster freedom.

Episodes from history in part one of this book strongly reinforce Rummel's conclusions. But this is not a history of atrocities committed by tyrants and despots, whose depressing stories have been told many times. I have focussed on the exploits of some of the "good men" of history, who are still highly regarded by the judgement of the years, but who found themselves in situations sufficiently desperate for them to resort to drastic measures to save the cause in which they believed.

We do not readily associate names like Julius Caesar, Emperor Justinian, Henry V of England, Pope Innocent III, Sir Thomas More, Napoleon, Horatio Nelson, Abraham Lincoln and Aung San Suu Kyi with brutality and extreme ruthlessness. But their stories all provide examples of what leaders sometimes feel compelled to do, in order to achieve what they regard as important.

In an era where fanaticism is on the rise in so many parts of the world, it is useful to examine the annals to try to understand what drives even civilised individuals to perpetrate atrocities. Even though the events occurred during the lifetime of many people who are alive today, we seem to have forgotten that inspirational leaders like Menachem Begin in Israel, Martin McGuiness in Ireland and Nelson Mandela in South Africa resorted to terrorist attacks on innocent civilians in attempts to overthrow the systems they opposed. Mahatma Gandhi was one of the few leaders who obtained independence for his country without advocating or openly resorting to violence. Gandhi's followers were prepared to go along with his non-violent, *satyagraha* philosophy when they were weak, but once they had achieved power, the whole country succumbed to sectarian violence. In 1947 and 1948, the Hindu-Muslim riots that preceded, accompanied and followed partition caused at least a million deaths.

Martin Luther King Jnr was the other great advocate of the non-violent protest although, like Gandhi, he despaired when many of his followers abandoned his approach. The words in one of his famous sermons are applicable to both parts of this book: "Human salvation lies in the hands of the creatively maladjusted."

For as long as we can find records, there have been leaders driven to do whatever it takes to achieve their aims, even though, as we will see, their actions in many cases trampled on the very standards and scruples they were fighting to uphold.

It is an approach which St. Paul condemns in his Epistle to the "Romans", ch.3 v.8: "that one should do evil that good may come of it". Yet many of the figures whose history you will read like Justinian, Charlemagne, Pope Innocent III, Thomas More and the people of Salem, invoked or at least sheltered behind deeply held Christian beliefs to justify their actions.

Other leaders like Caesar, Cromwell, Napoleon and Lincoln worked within established political frameworks to attain power, before assuming autocratic or absolute power for themselves. Henry V, Peter the Great and the relatively unknown Ranavalona profoundly changed their countries by ruthlessly exterminating rivals and threats. Our two great admirals Themistocles and Nelson were not the perpetrators of heinous crimes outside the din of war, but they were both prepared to ignore orders and customary standards of behaviour to achieve their successes

Our last character, Aung San Suu Kyi, has not gone out of her way to inflict evil in her native Burma, but she presides over a regime where atrocities are still being committed, without taking any effective action to contain the contagion that took the lives of so many and displaced hundreds of thousands.

To us, all their actions pose ethical questions. As Marcia Angell, the former editor of the *New England Journal of Medicine*, wrote: "Ethical violations are usually not a case of bad people doing bad things for no good reason; it is usually the case of good people doing bad things for good reasons." It is that distinction which underlies the examples chosen for this book.

I have not attempted to define what is wrong or right, nor to make value judgments about what was moral or immoral at the time of the events described (apart from a brief reference to notions of chivalry at the time of Henry V). I prefer the meta-ethical approach of addressing the foundations of morality, looking at what was done in the context of conventional beliefs, rather than by reference to particular views that then prevailed. People will always disagree about what is moral and immoral, but hopefully, most will always accept the fundamental standing of a morality of some sort. The murder of innocent civilians has been condemned by most societies in accordance with universal moral truths, and harsh laws have been enforced to prohibit such offences. What this book attempts to address is why such behaviour has so often been engaged in by individuals whose overall conduct was otherwise deserving of our admiration?

The history of humanity shows that most of us are compliant sheep, blithely following the common line. We are easy to lead and mislead. But amongst us there have always been numbers, mercifully small, of wolves happy to take advantage of our susceptibility in order to achieve the goals they consider important, happily sacrificing any number of sheep to attain them. Many of the wolves are inherently good. As Erich Fromm correctly notes, in order for the wolves to achieve their extremist aims, it is necessary for most sheep to have some wolf characteristics as well.

It was Sir Thomas More who presciently remarked in his book *Utopia* more than 500 years ago: "Your sheep that were wont to be so meek and tame, and so small eaters, now as I hear say, have become so great devourers, and so wild, that they eat up and swallow down the very men themselves."

The psychologist James Hollis posed the question and proffered some helpful answers in his book *Why Good People Do Bad Things*. Hollis emphasises that the human psyche is always divided and we delude ourselves when we think that we are in control of our "darker selves". He adopts the concept pioneered by Jung, of the "shadow" within us, that imbues us with a seductive energy, operating not only in our personal lives but in our political and social systems.

The "shadow" is not inherently evil, but the "charismatic madness" of a few can produce evil outcomes because the ordinary citizens can be cajoled, frightened or seduced into accepting what the righteous propose. The "righteous" in this case means those who are so convinced of the rightness of their own principles that they are prepared to impose them on others at whatever cost. Hollis makes the interesting observation that the greatest danger lies amongst the most righteous who uncritically believe that they are right, because they are the least capable of recognising the harm they bring to the world.

As he sees the situation, it is the erosion of the "old certainties" that has enabled fundamentalists and extremists to flourish, defying the nuanced achievements of scholarship and scientific evidence accumulated over the centuries.

For the purposes of what follows, I have assumed that there are actions and even wars that can legitimately be undertaken by any society when it perceives a threat to its existence or way of life. Much like the distinction that is embodied in the Geneva Convention, I have attempted to draw the line of what is unacceptable, by identifying situations where those in power have asserted the right to kill or otherwise mistreat their own people, or where, contrary to the rules of war, leaders have ruthlessly killed prisoners or innocent citizens.

I do not suggest that the essence of human beings is inherently good or particularly evil. But we represent a contradiction, with elements of both at work to varying degrees in everybody. In resolving our moral conflicts and dilemmas, we have a choice whenever we are called upon to deal with a dynamic situation, and it is up to us to decide which way we will act. It is important for us all to know that we have the choice, so that we can heed Plato's advice to avoid becoming so indifferent that evil will prevail by default because we fail to act. As Edmund Burke observed: "The only thing necessary for evil to triumph is for good men to do nothing."

Phillip Zimbardo is a professor of psychology who conducted a famous "prison experiment" at Stanford University in the summer of 1971, using randomly selected university students to act out the roles of prisoners and their guards. The relevance of his research is that even within the context of an experiment, the students who were dressed in uniforms to act as guards were so enamoured with their new found power over their fellow students, that the experiment had to be abandoned because the guards' brutal and sadistic treatment of the student prisoners was so realistic, that the prisoners became emotionally and psychologically traumatised by their experiences.

Reviewing his experiments more than 30 years later in 2007, Professor Zimbardo wrote: "Time had dimmed my memory of the creative evil in which many of the guards engaged, the extent of the suffering of many of the prisoners, and the extent of my passivity in allowing the abuses to continue for as long as I did—an evil of inaction."

Professor Zimbardo was as stunned by his own behaviour as by what he observed amongst his students, because he had become so caught up in his experiment that he was prepared to allow it to continue for six of the allocated fourteen days, even though it was obvious that a number of the prisoners were severely traumatised. Although the purpose of his research had been to expose the "authoritarian over-bearing boss-man", he himself had become one, in allowing the experiment to inflict real trauma.

Later admitting that the experiment had crossed the line into unethical conduct he wrote: "The negative power on which I had been running for the past week, had blinded me to the reality of the destructive impact of the System that I was sustaining." He concludes his 2007 book, *The Lucifer Effect*, by quoting from the former inmate of one of Stalin's gulags, Alexander Solzhenitsyn:

> The line between good and evil lies at the centre of every human heart.

Similar observations were made in the Milgram experiments at Yale University in the 1960s, when participants were encouraged by people in authority to administer increasingly dangerous electric shocks to victims when they answered questions incorrectly. Nearly two thirds of the randomly selected participants had no hesitation in raising the voltage levels from 15 volts up to the absolute maximum of 450 volts, even though they could hear the screams of their victims, apparently suffering severe pain or worse as a result of their actions.

Because those applying the electricity had been told they were serving science, they enthusiastically used the means at their disposal to inflict extreme torture on their fellow students, whose only offence was to provide incorrect answers to the questions asked. Fortunately for the Milgram participants, they were only acting out the role of victims who were not actually subjected to the shocks described, although those turning the dials were given every reason to believe they were.

Equally disturbing was research conducted by Professor David Buss at the University of Texas, who asked his students whether they had ever thought seriously about killing someone and if so, to write out their homicidal fantasies in an essay. Recent tragedies that continue to haunt America, have highlighted the relevance of Buss' research, disclosing that an astonishing 91% of the men and 84% of the women tested provided detailed and vivid homicidal fantasies, with a number also spelling out the steps they had taken to live out their fantasies in the real world. Although the students may have been vying for top marks in the course, the numbers are truly astounding.

In his article reviewing the research, David Brooks wrote: "We're natural-born killers and the real question is not what makes people kill, but what prevents them from doing so."

Studies conducted by another psychologist, Irving Staub, led him to conclude that "Evil that arises out of ordinary thinking and is committed by ordinary people is the norm, not the exception."

Such research establishes that we all have the potential to inflict evil on others and all we need for it to manifest itself is a clear vision of an enemy and the encouragement of someone in authority. We don't need to consume any of Dr Jekyll's mysterious potions, we are all capable of being transformed into the evil Mr Hyde if we let it happen.

The figures from history whose stories I have set out provide ample proof, because they were not evil, but merely determined to achieve their aims at whatever cost, because as they saw their situations, the ends justified whatever means were necessary.

In England in 1605, when the Gunpowder Plot was discovered just before the Houses of Parliament were about to be destroyed, Guy Fawkes said: "Desperate diseases call for desperate remedies."

A century earlier, the man who had been closest to Henry VIII—before falling out of favour with him, leading to his execution on the order of the King—Sir Thomas More, wrote of what mattered when dealing with heresy: "It is not the means by which the end is achieved, it is the justice of what is achieved at the end".

The attitude underlying both comments is reinforced by the episodes recorded in Part One of this book.

I will leave it to the reader to pass judgement on the conduct of people featured in this collection, and to rank them in order if you wish to gauge the relative heinousness of the distress, misery and deaths they caused. The closest I will stray in the direction of judgement is to point to the beliefs that were important to the perpetrators, in case they help provide benchmarks by which to measure the actions which were taken.

I am very much mindful of the current trend in historical biographies to denigrate and undermine the reputations of men previously held in high regard. The point was acknowledged by K.B. McFarlane when he wrote: "It pleases lesser mortals to detect the Achilles' heel of great ones that live in the world's eye."

Whilst the same accusation can be levelled against me, I have attempted to explain why the leaders I have chosen acted as they did, to try and preserve or achieve what they considered important. It may help us understand why they did it.

To include a moderate number of individuals, it has been necessary to give only an extremely abridged version of their lives, exposing this book to criticism for omitting part of the story. It might also be protested that I have not cited enough authorities to support the facts upon which I have relied. The two general propositions I advance to defend my approach are:

1. What follows is a genuine attempt to point out the key developments in the life of each individual and comprehend what each stood for and tried to achieve.

2. This is not intended as a scholarly work to settle academic disputes about factual details. It is intended to provide accessible and hopefully readable accounts, based on the best understanding of facts as I have been able to ascertain them. Any errors will be corrected in the next edition.

Many of the actions I recount would be condemned as deplorable and completely unacceptable by the standards of the 21st century. Yet because the objective was laudable or at least justifiable, history seems to accept the means by which it was achieved, as the price which had to be paid.

If we find it difficult, living in a stable, democratic society, to envisage the re-emergence of the behaviour I describe, there are clear indications that democracy is not working as well as its champions expected. Edward Luce has pointed out that in the decade prior to 2017, 25 democracies failed in different parts of the world. The increasingly autocratic regimes of Rodrigo Duterte in the Phillipines and Recep Erdogan in Turkey enjoy approval ratings that are the envy of elected leaders in the democracies of the West—where there is widespread disillusionment with the workings of elected governments and their bureaucracies. The life of Abraham Lincoln supplies an example of what extreme circumstances may lead to within a democratic framework. It would be naive in the extreme to suppose that what has happened before will not recur.

We therefore need to be mindful of the past in order to avoid the same mistakes. As Aldous Huxley famously remarked: "That men do not learn very much from the lessons of history, is the most important of all lessons history has to teach us."

The 16th century Italian writer and diplomat, Niccolo Machiavelli, analysed the ruthlessness of successful rulers in his book *Il Principe* (*The Prince*). I have started with him, not to champion his approach to the issues raised in this book, but because he is one of the few writers who has attempted to analyse and explain what drastic steps are sometimes necessary to enable an effective ruler to attain and preserve power.

It was Machiavelli who expressed the view reinforced by the examples from history which follow, namely that "Unless men are compelled to be good, they will invariably turn out bad." Machiavelli may not himself have perpetrated atrocities, but he argued in favour of such actions being taken when required, and the man he admired the most, Cesare Borgia, certainly took them.

Niccolo Machiavelli

[1469–1527]

Niccolo Machiavelli was born in Florence in 1469, the son of a lawyer whose career was blighted by tax debts, but who still found money for books. He passed his love of books on to his son Niccolo, whose career and fortune fluctuated with the power and influence of the Medici family. Having accumulated vast wealth as bankers, the Medicis dominated life in Florence for three generations. But after a disastrous military campaign against the city of Lucca, Cosimo Medici and the rest of his family were banished from Florence. During their absence, the young Machiavelli was appointed to senior posts, serving the city's government as Head of the Second Chancery and Secretary to the Council of Ten. He was sent as a young man on diplomatic missions to King Louis XII of France and Emperor Maximillian. When the Medicis returned to power, he was imprisoned and tortured, before being released and effectively banished from public life.

During this period in the political wilderness Machiavelli wrote a number of serious works, including most famously *Il Principe* (*The Prince*), based on observations of Cesare Borgia, the devious and ruthless son of Pope Alexander VI, who achieved considerable success in his attempt to unify Italy, until thwarted by the sudden death of his father in 1503 and his own death four years later.

Largely because they were constantly at war with one another, the prosperous city states of Italy were almost continuously under the control of foreign occupiers. It was Machiavelli's hope that a successful leader would emerge from the chaos of 16th century Italy, to unite the country against the invaders.

Although it is still debated whether Machiavelli intended his book to be a paean in praise of Borgia, or a more satirical critique of tyrannical rulers, my own view is that he was saddened by the continuing failure of powerful city states in Italy to throw off foreign conquerors and that he genuinely attempted a detailed analysis of what a ruler needs to understand in order to achieve and hold onto power.

Machiavelli's central theme was that in the real world, a prince will be surrounded by unscrupulous and ruthless rivals and enemies and must learn to compete with them, not by being virtuous or merciful, but by matching their ruthlessness. His approach was based on the premise of

adhering to what was most effective in acquiring and retaining power, unrestrained by ethical considerations, or concerns about what may be right or wrong.

He argued that it may be necessary to bamboozle and even delude the populace, in order to achieve what is in the best interests of the community and that the best way to defeat rivals and enemies is by isolating and weakening them and if necessary having them killed.

At his cynical best Machiavelli believed that it was better for a prince to be feared than loved, because love is fickle and unreliable. However he warned the prince against engendering hatred amongst his citizens. Success breeds respect and if a ruler is able to administer the state effectively, the citizenry will be prepared to tolerate any extreme measures that may be required. The leader should get others to perform unpleasant tasks so as not to erode his popularity, reserving to himself whatever actions make him look good. Opponents should either be appeased or crushed.

Later in this book, we will see examples of rulers who fall within Machiavelli's description of espousing the cause of liberty until they attain control, whereupon they are transformed into liberty's sworn enemies. "No sooner have they usurped authority, than they indulge in all manner of extreme injustice, cruelty and violence; this gives rise to laws and regulations whose sole objective, heedless of public good, is the furtherance of private gain."

To leap forward into the 21st century for a moment, it is interesting that despite the problems that still bedevil his country, Vladimir Putin used his background as a member of the KGB to instil fear into the citizens of Russia and has continued to wield largely unchallenged power there since 1999. In his alternating roles as Prime Minister and President, he has become one of the most astute and adept leaders on the world stage. He has outlasted everyone and was re-elected as President in March 2018, in breach of the Constitution, after celebrating his 65th birthday.

"Men should be either treated generously or destroyed, because they take revenge for slight injuries—for heavy ones they cannot." — Machiavelli

He has certainly put into practice what he publicly said Russia needed: "A strong government that would take responsibility for the rights of the individual and care for the society as a whole". Although there is a deliberate ambiguity in his statement, he makes it plain that it is the government that decides what rights the individual should be allowed, measured by what is good for society as a whole. Machiavelli would be proud of him.

When writing about Livy's books on the history of Rome, Machiavelli expressed his views of statehood: "It is necessary for him who lays out a state and arranges law for it to presuppose that all men are evil and that they are always going to act according to the wickedness of their spirits whenever they have free scope." He added that "Men should be either treated generously or destroyed, because they take revenge for slight injuries—for heavy ones they cannot."

On 23 May 1498, the young Machiavelli watched from his office in the Palazzo Vecchio, as the monk Savonarola was burnt at the stake, bringing to an end "The Dictatorship of God", a period of religious extremism in Florence. The experience caused Machiavelli later to write: "Unarmed prophets always come to a sorry end."

Savonarola had been a fanatic of religion, whereas Machiavelli was a fanatic of power. After unsuccessful attempts to achieve power for himself, Machiavelli accepted a lesser role as counsellor to Pietro Soderini, who was elected as the Republic's Gonfalonier (Florence's head of state) for life in 1502. At 33 years of age, Machiavelli found himself at the centre of political life in the city of his birth, and although his name is today synonymous with political ruthlessness and underhand dealings, his advice to Florence's leader at the time appears to have been balanced and generally sensible. He wrote most of the Gonfalonier's most memorable speeches and was instrumental in successfully negotiating with the numerous foreign and Italian potentates who harboured ambitions of acquiring the wealth of Florence.

He was no saint however in his personal life and was frequently found with prostitutes and gamblers, whose society he preferred to the company of princes and kings with whom he had to negotiate. He had a particular enthusiasm for a prostitute called *La Riccia* and he often arranged mistresses in each city he visited in the course of his duties, despite being married for most of his adult life to Marietta, who bore him several children.

By 1507, he held three senior positions in the government of the Republic and had established himself as the most erudite and skilful of all the city's advisers. He realised that with its reliance on foreign mercenaries, who were both expensive and unreliable, Florence would always be vulnerable to attack and dependent on shaky alliances with foreign powers. The newly elected Pope, Julius II, wasted no time in pursuing an aggressive conquest of large areas of northern Italy and his Spanish allies succeeded in storming the Florentine fortress of Prato before slaughtering most of its inhabitants.

The Papist forces took control of Florence and unsurprisingly Machiavelli was dismissed from all his offices when the Medici family returned to power in 1512. He was imprisoned and tortured by being subjected to the *strappado*, during which his hands were tied behind his back and lifted high in the air before being dropped almost to the ground six times. Whilst in jail, he penned a clever sonnet which he sent to Giuliano de' Medici, whose brother had just been elected as Pope Leo X on 9 March 1513 after the death of Julius.

Machiavelli was eventually released and permitted to retire to a modest rural property outside the city, where he dedicated himself to literature and writing for the last 15 years of his life. The books upon which his later reputation was based were mostly not published till after his death, but Machiavelli had firsthand experience in the workings of government in 16th century Florence and could carefully observe what was needed for a ruler to be successful. He discarded his work clothes and dressed himself in the regal garments of court life before sitting down to write. In a letter to his friend Francesco Vettori on 10 December 1513 he wrote "And for four hours at a time I feel no boredom, I forget my troubles, I do not dread poverty, and I am not afraid of death. I absorb myself into them completely."

His book *The Art of War* was published during his lifetime and read by some of Florence's leaders but its message was not heeded. Although he was permitted to present a copy of *The Prince* to the young Lorenzo di Piero de' Medici, that prince was more absorbed in some hunting dogs given to him at the same time, and apparently never bothered to read Machiavelli's masterpiece.

Machiavelli also wrote two comic plays, the first of which *Mandragola* achieved some success despite its scandalous content. It even found favour with Pope Leo who was prepared to overlook its denigration of the Church. The second *Clizia* was inspired by a beautiful young actress, Barbara Raffacani, who starred in the production and was to be Machiavelli's frequent companion during his last three years.

His political writings display a profound knowledge of antiquity and a reverence for classical learning as well as a perceptive analysis of the eternal conflict between the ruler and the ruled. He defended the violence and tumult of ancient Rome as being the necessary breeding ground for what inspired the Roman Republic to achieve such outstanding success in war and conquest. He expressed provocative views disparaging the role of Christianity in softening and diluting the hard edge that successful politicians needed. More importantly he viewed the church's role in honouring weakness and celebrating humility, as having a tranquilising effect on citizens, making them more vulnerable to being subjugated by tyrants.

Machiavelli denounced the city's reliance on auxiliaries and foreign mercenaries and was instrumental in introducing and training a new citizen militia, drawn from the young men of the city and the surrounding areas who would free the Republic from its reliance on corrupt and dishonest soldiers of fortune. He argued that Florence would be more secure with its own soldiers with sword at the ready, than relying on someone else's sword to defend the city. He urged young men not to ask what their city could do for them but, like the youth of ancient Athens, what they might do for their city. Nearly 500 years later, President Kennedy borrowed that simple philosophy in his inaugural address on 20 January 1961.

Machiavelli advocated the use of visual horror depicting war as cruel and violent, to prepare citizens for wars which he regarded as inevitable. His philosophy was graphically depicted in the work which Leonardo da Vinci was commissioned to paint on the wall of the Great Council Hall in Florence celebrating *The Battle of Anghiari.* Although the mural was never completed and has not survived, we can still see the sketches and cartoons the great artist prepared for the mural, which portray the full horror of war bursting with fury and violence.

Following the publication of Machiavelli's poem *Decennale* in 1506, the other great Renaissance artist at work in Florence, Michelangelo, produced an equally powerful painting symbolising the philosophy espoused by Machiavelli, in which we see a young Florentine soldier, clad in armour with sword in hand, standing in front of the Piazza della Signoria with a distant view of the artist's statue of David, standing at the ready to take on the giant Goliath.

In waging war, Machiavelli recommended successful tactics for a town under siege:

- Having made adequate preparations, convince the citizens the siege will be short.
- Remind them of the cruelty of the enemy.
- Introduce strict controls over the population because of the emergency.

He firmly believed that so long as the people could see that the measures were for their benefit in the longer term, they would tolerate even acts of evil. "The only thing one owes the people is results," he wrote; the only vices a prince needs to avoid are those that would destroy his power.

He accepted that men will always be attracted to the idea of a change in the status quo, so long as they can see themselves as benefitting from it, even though life tells us that often in replacing a bad system there is a risk of finishing with something even worse. Greed predominates in a world where men always see things as they wish them to be, rather than as they actually are.

He expressed an opinion central to the thread that permeates this part of the book, when he exhorted the prince to hold to what is right when he can, but know how to do wrong when he must.

He was commissioned to write a history of Florence which he completed just before his death on 22 June 1527, but was otherwise largely banished from any active role in Florence. He belatedly received some recognition in his final years, but was powerless to change what was happening when Rome was brutally sacked by the army of Charles V in 1527. By this time he was seriously ill and died on 21 June 1527, soon after his return to Florence.

Machiavelli realised that the coming of artillery not only made it necessary to reorganise completely the defences of towns and cities, but also brought all concepts of chivalry and picturesque knights to an abrupt end. He has been harshly judged by history as a result of a somewhat distorted interpretation of his ideas. His name has been unfairly associated with duplicity and baseless violence, but it is more accurate to say that he believed in a transparent exercise of power, where harsh measures are only taken as a last resort, when no other course is open to ward off even greater evils.

He was severe in his criticism of the Catholic Church, partly because of the hypocrisy of so many of its cardinals and even popes, who were as debauched as anyone in Italy, but he also believed that its focus on the after-life distracted people from dealing with reality. As he wrote in *The Prince*: "he who neglects what is done for what ought to be done, sooner effects his ruin than his preservation; for a man who wishes to act entirely up to his professions of virtue soon meets with what destroys him among so much that is evil."

He was a brilliant writer and political analyst, who wrote with exceptional skill, providing insights that are still relevant today. It is difficult to think of any other figure in history who contributed so many original ideas to the study of statecraft.

Unlike most of his contemporaries, he did not seek to benefit from the power he wielded, and both his actions and the advice that he gave were always founded on what he believed was in the best interests of the city and country he undoubtedly loved. As he recorded in a letter to a friend late in his life: "My poverty is a witness to my honesty."

Although his writings seem to have had only limited influence on events in Italy, I strongly suspect that men like Napoleon and more recently Putin adopted his approach. Thomas Cromwell, who was so influential in sending Sir Thomas More to his death, had definitely absorbed the Machiavellian approach during his stay in Italy. Former US President Bill Clinton was reported to have slept with a copy of Machiavelli's book on his bedside table.

What Michael White wrote in his recent book on Machiavelli will be borne out by the characters we examine: "Machiavelli did not invent Machiavellianism, he observed it and as long as humans are humans, they will behave in the way he described."

Julius Caesar

[100 BC–44 BC]

Julius Caesar was born on 13 July 100BC, into a noble and highly respected Roman family. His father had served as a senator and his mother Aurelia Cotta hailed from a family of consuls on both sides. Although we know very little about his early years, his father died when he was only 16 and as a 19 year old, he received the Civic Crown, one of Rome's highest awards for bravery, after personally saving the life of the governor at the siege of Mytilene. However, the young Caesar sided with his uncle Marius in the civil war against the ultimately victorious Sulla, causing him to be stripped of his inheritance, and compelled to spend time in exile on the island of Rhodes.

He was soon back in Rome practising his oratory as an advocate in the law courts, and serving as an aedile, a praetor, and then Pontifex Maximus—senior elected positions under Rome's republican constitution. Eventually he became a consul. Consuls were the executive leaders of the state. Because of the anti-monarchical principle in the ancient constitution, consuls had to serve two at a time, and step down after one year.

Afterwards, in his first military command, as governor of Spain in 61BC, Caesar succeeded in imposing Roman rule over vast new territories. Returning to Rome a year later, he was sufficiently powerful to join the First Triumvirate, sharing de facto rule of the Empire with Pompey and Crassus, before being posted to what is now France, to subdue the Gallic tribes.

Caesar spent eight years away from Rome, during which time he conquered the whole of Gaul and much of Britain as well as repelling the Germanic tribes back across the Rhine in a brilliantly successful and very well remunerated campaign. Much of the popular glory attached to his name arose from the carefully crafted summaries of his successes that can still be read today in his book *The Gallic Wars*. Latin students all over the world have been prescribed his lucid prose as a text to advance their studies. He also wrote poetry that was greatly admired.

Although only slightly built he was mentally and physically agile and he often led his soldiers into the heat of battle even when he was in his fifties. He suffered from epilepsy, which those closest to him sometimes had to disguise. General Wesley Clark said of Caesar in one of the most recent biographies:

> it was his tactical acumen, strategic brilliance and insights that made him unique . . . He had to maneuver [sic] his way to the top. And then, even while engaged in combat, battles and campaigns on Rome's frontiers, he kept his footing in the slippery politics of Rome, first by forging alliances, and then by, as a last resort, engaging in civil war against envious, jealous rivals. He was about power and he used every tool and means at his disposal, including the vast personal wealth gained by his conquests, to achieve and maintain his growing power.

Even Cicero, one of his staunchest critics at the time, was prepared to acknowledge that "his character was an amalgamation of genius, method, memory, culture, thoroughness, intellect and industry."

Before his time in Gaul, Cesar was deeply in debt, maintaining his appeal to the masses with extravagant celebrations he could not afford. He was also a serial adulterer who regularly seduced the wives of other men. On the death of his wife Cornelia in 69BC, he nevertheless arranged an unprecedented celebration of her life, with a dazzling programme of games and spectacles, greatly enhancing his public profile. His second marriage was to Sulla's granddaughter, whom he later divorced because of her alleged infidelity, famously saying: "Caesar's wife must be above suspicion," notwithstanding her husband's notorious philandering.

An earlier episode illustrates why Caesar and the Romans generally were so successful. Returning from the siege of Miletus in the Eastern Mediterranean, the young man who would become one of Rome's greatest generals was captured by pirates near the island of Pharmacussa. After Caesar demanded that his ransom be doubled to properly reflect his status, the money was duly paid by his family and the Roman Senate, and he was released.

Before leaving his captors however, he promised that he would have his revenge and without even returning to Rome, he recruited and trained a new force of legionaries, and pursued the pirates to the island of Samos, where he had them all crucified, keeping most of the re-captured ransom monies for himself and his recruits, as well as the substantial haul of other booty that the pirates had accumulated.

Although he returned to Northern Italy after successes in Gaul in both 57BC and 56BC, the continued rebellions of the Gauls compelled his return. For those Gallic and Belgian tribes who sued for peace, Caesar was generous and supportive, demanding hostages and unconditional surrender, but exacting no revenge. But for tribes like the Advantuci and Veneti who continued to resist the Roman invasion, he was ruthless, killing their leaders and selling whole populations into slavery, often razing their towns to the ground.

Much to the amazement of the barbarians, Caesar's engineers managed to erect a bridge across the Rhine in only ten days, enabling him to pursue the Germans deep into their own territory, before returning to the western bank of the river and demolishing the bridge. He also completed two successful invasions of Britain, but the extreme poverty of the inhabitants did not yield the booty he expected and he returned to Gaul in 54BC.

The last serious challenge to Roman rule occurred under the inspired leadership of Vercingetorix, who united the Gallic tribes more than ever before. After a protracted siege of Avaricum and the decisive battle of Alesia, Vercingetorix himself surrendered to Caesar, later to be led in chains before the Roman people in Caesar's triumph. Gaul was finally subdued. He had forced the surrender of 800 cities and subdued 300 warlike nations whilst acquiring vast wealth in the process—it was understandable that his rivals in Rome were intensely jealous.

Of course "Big Julie's" most famous *Whatever it Takes* moment occurred when he returned to Italy after his brilliantly successful campaign as the governor of Gaul. In his absence, Rome had been overrun, with electoral chaos and gang violence playing into the hands of the ambitious Pompey, who had himself elected as sole Consul early in 52BC.

Caesar's former partners in power attempted to emulate his popular successes. However, Crassus was killed in the battle of Carrhae and Pompey's military failures made him only more determined to defeat Caesar, particularly after the death of Julia, Caesar's only daughter, who had been Pompey's wife.

Caesar and his victorious legions reached Ravenna where he was informed that his former ally Pompey had become so envious of his success, that he had persuaded the Senate to divest Caesar of all power by requiring him to return to Rome alone and unarmed as he would otherwise be declared an "enemy of the state". Roman law rendered it an act of treason for any man to enter Italy across the River Rubicon with a standing army.

Caesar made some conciliatory offers to try to resolve the situation, however all attempts at a negotiated settlement failed and after some hesitation Caesar decided to cross the river with his fully armed and battle hardened 23rd Legion on 20 January 49BC.

As the scene was described by the Roman historian Suetonius, Caesar contemplated the Rubicon for some time, before snatching a trumpet from one of his soldiers and sounding the "Advance" with a piercing blast. He then crossed the small bridge after crying out: "Let us go where the omens of the Gods and the crimes of our enemies summon us. The die is cast."

So although Caesar was a trained lawyer, who clearly knew that his action amounted to blatant defiance against the Senate of the Roman people, plunging the country again into civil war in which Romans would slaughter Romans in their thousands, he felt compelled to take the action he did because of the circumstances that confronted him.

After capturing Ariminum almost without bloodshed, Caesar marched on Rome to find that Pompey and many of the Senators had deserted it, retreating to Brundisium and eventually Greece, enabling Caesar to seize control of the whole of Italy within 60 days. He invited exiles back to Rome without punishment and arranged for laws to be passed to relieve the burdens of debt. He even resigned the dictatorship to enable him to continue in his pursuit of Pompey.

He followed Pompey to Greece where, after initially suffering a defeat at Petra, he quickly recovered with reinforcements and achieved a decisive victory at the battle of Pharsalus. Unlike Pompey, he did not hesitate to pursue the soldiers of the defeated army until they were either killed or surrendered to his cause. Wherever possible he spared the lives of those who fought against him, even though some of the opposing legionaries had fought alongside him in earlier campaigns.

He then pursued Pompey to Egypt where the Egyptians presented his severed head to a horrified Caesar. After his defeat of Pompey, Caesar viewed the corpses of the Roman soldiers who had been killed in the conflict and said: "They would have it so. Even I, Gaius Caesar, after my great achievements, would have been convicted in the courts, had I not sought help from my army."

Whilst in Egypt, Caesar became completely besotted with the Egyptian Princess Cleopatra, whom he installed as the new Queen of Egypt, the last of the monarchs descended from Ptolemy, who had ruled Egypt since the time of Alexander the Great. She later gave birth to Caesar's only known son, who briefly ruled Egypt as Ptolemy XV, before being killed on the orders of Caesar's successor Octavian.

"his character was an amalgamation of genius, method, memory, culture, thoroughness, intellect and industry." — Cicero

---

After returning to Rome in 46BC, he began introducing reforms of the political system. He also reformed the calendar, introducing a 365 day year, with a leap year every fourth year, bringing the lunar and solar year into a unified system for the first time in history. He began assuming greater power as he bypassed the Senate, by designating governors, appointing many of the senior office holders and exercising personal executive and legislative jurisdiction. As Plutarch described the situation: "The most open and deadly hatred towards him was produced by his passion for the royal power."

Although repeatedly warned that there were plots against his life, Caesar refused to accept a bodyguard, saying "It is better to suffer death once, than always to live in fear." He put in place plans to dig a ship canal through the Isthmus of Corinth, and to drain marshes and divert the Tiber so as to allow the merchant ships easy access to the city of Rome from a new harbour at Ostia.

Before embarking on yet another military campaign, Caesar arranged for his own appointment as *Dictator Perpetuus* ("dictator without term"), a breach of the constitution which infuriated his enemies even more. Little wonder that he survived only six months in Rome after returning from his final victory in Spain, before his rivals murdered him on the floor of the Senate on 15 March 44BC, beneath the statue of his old nemesis Pompey. Of the 23 dagger wounds found on his body, only one that penetrated close to his heart gave him the speedy death he had always hoped would be his fate.

The conspirators who murdered Caesar would have us believe that they acted out of a love of liberty and of their country, in hoping to restore Rome to a republic. It is likely that they had a variety of motivations, driven by the outstanding success Caesar had achieved to act out of envy, personal pique and even in an attempt to achieve similar power for themselves. Caesar had never attempted to ingratiate himself with those who plotted against him and although he was loved by the common people, he loved power even more.

He was one of Rome's greatest generals, who achieved outstanding successes on the battlefield, as the inspirational leader of legionaries who were devoted to him. He also introduced reforms of the civil systems in Rome, which had become increasingly corrupt. But his ambitions were always more personal than civic minded and the absolute power he came to wield made his demise almost inevitable, in a city that had not yet rejected its republican traditions.

In his memorable speech after the assassination, Mark Antony turned the populace against the murderers, by revealing that the man they had killed had left a will in which he bequeathed his gardens to the people as an area of public recreation and had provided for a payment of 75 drachma to every Roman citizen. It is interesting to speculate whether events would have turned out differently if such provisions had been disclosed before his death.

Far from assisting the cause of restoring the Republic, the murderers only brought about its downfall as well as their own demise, as first Mark Antony and later the young Octavian assumed power in the first of a long line of Roman Emperors. Everyone involved in Caesar's death was pursued and killed including Brutus and Cassius who were compelled to take their own lives.

As always, the victors are best placed to demonise the vanquished and Shakespeare was probably correct in his play "Julius Caesar", when he wrote:

> The evil that men do lives after them,
> The good is oft' interred with their bones.

Emperor Justinian I

[482–565]

The man who would become one of the greatest emperors to rule the Roman Empire in the East was born Flavius Petrus Sabbatius in a humble peasant household, not far from Skopje in Illyria (modern day Macedonia). His uncle Justin had recognised his nephew's talents at a young age and after having himself been unexpectedly appointed Emperor from amongst the ranks of the Imperial Guard at age 66, he arranged for the youthful Justinian to be educated in Constantinople, where he was groomed to ascend the imperial throne.

Justinian was appointed Consul in 521 and as his uncle began to display increasing signs of senility, Justinian progressively assumed effective control. Justinian had used his influence to have a law passed repealing an ancient prohibition on senators marrying stage performers so he could marry the great love of his life, Theodora, who had formerly worked as a courtesan performing lewd stage acts. And so after Justin died in 527, Justinian was crowned in Constantinople on 4 April as the new Emperor, and Theodora as Empress.

We still see the two of them portrayed with their retinues, in glorious gold-covered mosaics as they stare lovingly at each other across the altar of the San Vitale church in Ravenna. Although an impressive figure for a man by then in his sixties, the Emperor nevertheless appears as an ordinary looking, round-faced man, illuminated only by piercing eyes.

After his coronation, Justinian immediately embarked upon an ambitious and largely successful campaign to restore the shrunken Roman Empire to its ancient boundaries. His outstanding generals Belisarius and Narses were able to deal firstly with the Persians, followed by the conquest of North Africa, Sicily, and extensive areas of Italy and even Spain. They recovered the city of Rome and fought successful campaigns against the Vandals and the Ostrogoths. While the campaigns strained the resources of the Empire, they expanded Justinian's power into vast new territories. Although there were still frequent incursions by the barbarian tribes to the north, Justinian established a series of fortified positions along the banks of the Danube to give some protection to the empire.

Chronic water shortages in Constantinople, combined with the threat of the city's aqueduct being destroyed by any invading army, led

Justinian to construct a magnificent underground water cistern in the heart of the city that still attracts thousands of tourists today. It is 460 feet long, 230 feet wide, with a 26 feet high roof supported by 336 columns carved in stone.

Even more ambitious and enduring in significance, was the enormous task undertaken by Justinian and his legal draftsmen, to simplify, unify and codify the complex and confusing agglomeration of laws that had developed over the centuries. Irrelevant and anomalous provisions were repealed to compile a single set of laws into the *Corpus Iuris Civilis* ("The Code of Civil Law"), which still forms the basis of the civil law systems administered throughout most of Europe apart from the UK. Like Roman law over the centuries, most of Justinian's legislation was issued in Latin, but later in his reign, he began to issue laws in Greek, which undoubtedly contributed to the decline in the use of Latin.

The importance of the Code was not only to codify the law into a unified and coherent body of jurisprudence applied throughout the empire. With the approved commentaries, it also made the law transparent and accessible, laying the foundation for a comprehensible legal system that is still employed 1,500 years later.

His rule did not go unchallenged and his attempts to reduce the mounting burden of government spending were unpopular. When the execution of two criminals was botched in 532, the two factions of Blue and Green who packed into the Hippodrome for the chariot races each day, united in their opposition to the Emperor, even going so far as to crown one of their number as a new emperor. The protest soon morphed into riots followed by a full scale rebellion dubbed *Nika*, meaning Victory. Many churches and public buildings were engulfed by fire as large swathes of the city were destroyed.

After making an unsuccessful attempt to calm the mob, Justinian was tempted to flee the capital, but was persuaded to stay by Theodora and his faithful general Belisarius. Eventually Justinian ordered his army into the Hippodrome resulting in the massacre of 30,000 to 35,000 largely unarmed civilians.

Amongst the many buildings which had been destroyed by the rebels was the ancient basilica of Aghia Sophia ("Holy Wisdom"). Showing his customary energy and organisational skills, Justinian assembled an army of architects and builders to design and construct a new church which was built on a scale that dwarfed everything before it. Completed in less than six years after the rebellion, the Aghia Sophia church still dominates the skyline of modern Istanbul along with the Blue Mosque built nearly a thousand years later. It must have been truly astonishing for visitors in the 6th century, with a dome 31 metres in diameter, suspended 55 metres from its base and pierced by 40 windows to illuminate its enormous interiors. Adorned with stunning mosaic tiles and marble of every colour, the church also incorporated a great clock fitted with 24 doors that opened and closed to mark the hours. What a sight it must have been and although its dome did collapse on occasions during severe earthquakes, it was always rebuilt and its splendour has in no way been diminished by the four minarets that were added to it after 1453, to convert the original Christian structure to the cause of Islam.

Paul the Silentiary remarked in one of his poems:

> In the great church, Justinian outstrips Rome.

Justinian expanded his own palace, cascading downhill to the water of the Bosporus. He enjoyed the palace so much that he rarely left it during his reign of nearly 40 years. Many other churches and public buildings were restored or built from scratch throughout the city and the empire. The Emperor's ego caused him to rename no less than 27 cities after himself. He constructed huge numbers of fortresses to protect the Empire as well as monasteries to expand the learning of all citizens within his desired religious framework. Under Justinian's rule, most of the Byzantine elite became literate, with even career soldiers and bureaucrats writing important books.

The incursions of barbarians continued, and one Hun army reached the walls of the city. There were also numerous earthquakes and worst of all the arrival of the bubonic plague in 542, which devastated whole cities and left farms with no-one to work them. It is estimated that more than ten million lives were lost to the insidious disease spread by flea-infested rats. In the city, up to 5,000 people a day were dying in excruciating pain. The number of bodies became so overwhelming that the tops of the towers defending the city were removed so the towers could be filled with corpses.

Some of his contemporaries blamed the Emperor for the calamities that beset the empire. Yet Justinian overcame all the challenges thrown at him, and although history has judged some of his actions harshly, he was a great leader who changed the world profoundly.

The glorious achievements of his long reign were meticulously recorded in the official works of paid writers such as Marcellinus and Procopius, both of whom wrote of the Emperor in glowing terms. Procopius, however, secretly used his spare time to record his real feelings about his master and the Empress, in a work that is now much more widely read than the official histories, since it came to light in the 17th century.

Procopius' book *The Secret History* recorded in vicious and scandalous terms what Procopius regarded as the true character of the Emperor and his wife, describing him as a man "with no more sense than a donkey, ready to follow anyone who pulled the rein, waving its ears all the time". Justinian was, according to Procopius, "an extraordinary mixture of folly and wickedness inseparably blended . . . he was passionately devoted to murder and plunder; quarrelsome and subversive in the extreme."

Despite his reputation as a lawmaker, Procopius describes him as someone who either ignored the law or twisted it to his advantage and who was completely under the powerful influence of the evil and corrupt Empress.

Justinian promulgated laws prohibiting illicit payments to judicial officers, yet Procopius accuses him of being "an unstable weather-cock" who failed to uphold the laws he introduced, with the scales of justice usually tipped in favour of the party paying the most gold.

Procopius admits that he was extremely energetic and hard working, surviving on only a few hours of sleep each night. Procopius also describes him as always approachable and affable in dealings with his subjects, but heartless and cruel beyond measure when dealing with his enemies.

The book undoubtedly includes many tales that were heavily embellished and in some cases, probably invented, but the details cannot be completely dismissed and it has endured partly because it presents such a contrasting picture to the official histories. The truth probably lies between the two. Justinian displayed sufficient ruthlessness in achieving his success to render him not quite the paradigm of virtue and integrity that the official versions recount.

Before Justinian was crowned his rival for the throne, Vitalian, was murdered by being stabbed 16 times in the imperial palace, along with his two aides. Although they were not directly implicated, it is thought that Justinian and/or his uncle were probably behind the assassination.

After his coronation, Justinian's deeply held Christian beliefs inspired him to apply his vast energy in an attempt to unify the church and rid it of the schisms and heresies that bedevilled it in different areas of the empire. He assembled opposing factions at the palace of Hormisdas for three days of debate, while the city was still smouldering from the Nika riots. His attempts to achieve compromise, however, were unsuccessful and he became sufficiently irritated by the intransigence of those opposed to the Chalcedonian doctrines he embraced that he foolishly attempted to impose his will by force, despite the fact that Theodora herself strongly supported the Monophysite heresy which he opposed.

Bishops of Syria, Egypt and other places simply insisted on consecrating more members of the clergy sympathetic to their beliefs, despite all the Emperor's attempts to impose his own doctrines. Far from achieving uniformity of dogma, the church became even more fragmented.

In political and diplomatic endeavours, he was much more successful. Although not a great orator, he was highly effective in using his skills as a communicator to unify his allies and set the enemies of the Empire against each other. However it should be noted that Procopius says

Justinian squandered much of the wealth he had inherited from his predecessors in attempting to buy off foes.

His opposition to traditions and practices he considered inconsistent with his Christian beliefs prompted him to take extreme actions against dissident groups including lawyers, bureaucrats and noblemen. He wielded his authority in Athens where philosophers from all over the world had continued to gather in the academies of Plato and Aristotle for more than a thousand years. Justinian prohibited the teaching of philosophy because it encouraged heresy, saying "Thus we permit only holders of the orthodox faith to teach and be paid from public funds." The academies were closed in 529AD and most of the philosophers moved to cities outside his control.

Justinian was able to reform the political systems of the empire by removing much of the corruption and centralising its control. His choices for senior positions in the army and the law and the architects of his enormous building programmes were inspired selections. They worked quickly and efficiently to implement the emperor's ambitious projects. One of his key appointments to work on the Civil Code, was Tribonian, whose legal acumen demanded that his services be retained, even though he had played a pivotal role in the Nika rebellion.

"no more sense than a donkey, ready to follow anyone who pulled the rein, waving its ears all the time" — Procopius

---

Justinian created grand visions and yet he was frequently obsessed with petty jealousies. He was the driving force behind most of the great achievements of the empire during his rule, but he alienated many by his ruthlessness.

The wars his generals almost continuously waged were costly and most of the expansion of the empire they succeeded in achieving was of brief duration.

Justinian's long reign was one of the most successful periods in the history of the Eastern Roman Empire. Magnificent buildings were created, its territories expanded and laws were unified. As the Nika rebellion and the Hormisdas conclave demonstrate, he consistently attempted to resolve conflicts by conciliation or compromise. But like many strong leaders, he resorted to extreme measures to achieve his objectives when opponents attempted to stand in his way.

If he had been less committed to enforcing his will in religious and military matters, he may have enjoyed more success in creating an enduring and united empire. As it was, he was so sure of his own immortality, that when he was on his deathbed without an heir, he left it till his last day before nominating his nephew Justin as his successor. Much of what he had achieved disintegrated within a generation of his death on 14 November 565.

Emperor Charlemagne

[742–814 AD]

Although he lived long after the collapse of the Roman Empire in Western Europe, and more than 200 years after Justinian's rule, as King of the Franks, Charlemagne established what was dubbed the Holy Roman Empire, that stretched from his native Francia to the Baltic Sea, into Germany, Spain, Italy, Bohemia and as far east as the Slavic kingdoms in the Danube Basin. In fact, as Voltaire famously pointed out, it was neither Holy nor Roman, but Charlemagne's energy and considerable skills succeeded in imposing his Christian beliefs on all the areas he conquered.

On the death of King Pepin III, his elder son Charlemagne inherited half his kingdom. Charlemagne became the sole ruler when his younger brother died in 771. He then achieved almost immediate success by taking over the Lombard Kingdom in Northern Italy. However, his attempts to conquer and convert Saxony required his attention for more than 30 years of intermittent warfare. He established his capital in Aachen (Aix-la-Chapelle), where he promoted education, architecture and the arts in an attempt to unify Europe and create a refined and prosperous society in what became known as the Carolingian Renaissance.

His reforms were instrumental in helping the area of modern day Europe to emerge from the Dark Ages after the collapse of the original Roman Empire, laying the religious, cultural and artistic foundations for Western Civilisation.

By improving the education of the clergy, he not only helped spread the Christian faith through monastic schools, but also created an effective system for administering the vast area of his new empire, through a network of bishops. Despite the expensive wars he continued to wage, the empire did not impose taxes on its citizens. He expanded the role and standing of the biennial meetings of the *Placitum Generale* assembly, to unite and work with both the ecclesiastical and the secular lords, allowing even dissenting voices to be heard.

After inviting prominent intellectuals from all the major centres to his capital at Aachen, he established mediaeval Latin as the language of literature, the church and the law. Many ancient texts, including those by classical writers like Virgil, Horace and Plato, survive today because

of copies made of them during the Carolingian Renaissance. Charlemagne was a great patron of art and architecture, constructing many cathedrals, monasteries and civic buildings all over the Empire. He established diplomatic ties with the Caliphate of Baghdad and the Eastern Roman Empire. Public education was introduced, with a palace school for the children of aristocrats established in the capital, and many other schools established in monasteries with considerable libraries assembled from all over the Empire.

He had four wives we know of and when the last wife Liutgard died in 800, he had a succession of mistresses adding to his already impressive number of progeny. Despite his notorious love of feasting Charlemagne insisted upon strict adherence to the letter of divine law, with his overriding concern always being to identify the right course and stick to it at all costs. He was intent on removing superstition from religion, to restore harmony and reason to its tarnished reputation. Although he struggled to write, he introduced a uniform and more legible script for writing and levels of literacy rose under his rule.

He established public law courts, to which even peasants had access, with royal representatives, called *missi*, operating circuit courts to adjudicate local disputes with commendable impartiality. He also issued and attempted to enforce throughout the Empire a uniform system of laws, called *capitula*, including a "General Admonition" in 789, which not only outlawed corruption and abuse of power, but emphasised the importance of upholding moral standards as well as the need for peaceful resolution of disputes and the general avoidance of sin.

When Charlemagne's son, the future King Louis the Pius, was found to have transgressed the Royal Decree, even he was required to perform a public penance for his wrongdoing.

Refusal to accept baptism was punishable by death.

During the 46 years of his reign, there were no less than 60 military expeditions, half of them led by Charlemagne himself. Amongst the territories he conquered and theoretically converted to Christianity were large areas of Germany, Bavaria and Saxony. The Saxons were stubbornly resistant to the new religion and their rebellion resulted in the defeat of one of Charlemagne's armies at Suntelberg. Although he may have intended originally to absorb the Saxons into his Empire without undue bloodshed, their raids upon monasteries in the Rhine district and repeated breaking of treaties led to more than 30 years of warfare during which the level of violence gradually escalated. The all-conquering King wielded a sword with a cross-shaped hilt "at the ready for attacking pagans".

Like later crusader armies, Charlemagne firmly believed that Christ's admonition, "Love thy neighbour", applied only to Christian neighbours, and he proceeded to suppress the Saxon rebellion ruthlessly. It culminated in the beheading of 4,500 Saxon prisoners at Verden, who refused his generous offer of being baptised. He introduced the "Saxon Capitulary", under which paganism was exterminated. Refusal to accept baptism was punishable by death. Crippling fines were imposed for failure to have a child baptised and cremation of a corpse was made a capital offence. With the stroke of a pen, paganism had been banned and at the point of a sword every aspect of Saxon life was transformed.

After being invited to Rome by Pope Leo III, Charlemagne was crowned Emperor on Christmas Day 800, before the shrine of St. Peter, to honour the vast expansion in the population of Christians that followed Charlemagne's military successes. By the time Charlemagne was succeeded as Emperor by his son Louis the Pius in 814, he had established and pacified an empire that was the biggest in Western Europe until the era of Napoleon, nearly a thousand years later.

Although we know him by his French name, Charlemagne actually spoke in a German dialect and he is still commemorated in Germany as Emperor Charles the Great. The Holy Roman Empire he founded endured for nearly a thousand years, before it was finally dissolved in 1806. When Napoleon crowned himself as Emperor of France in 1804, he placed on his own head a copy of Charlemagne's crown, because the Viennese steadfastly refused to allow the original to be transported to France.

Like many dominant leaders, Charlemagne was followed after death by successors who could not emulate, nor even preserve his achievements. During their reigns his empire began to fragment, in part at least because he and his successors failed to heed the advice of the great Anglo-Saxon scholar, Alcuin: "faith comes of free will, not of compulsion. How can a man be compelled to believe what he does not believe? You may force a man to the font, but not to the faith."

Pope Innocent III

[1161–1216]

Innocent III was one of the most ruthless and successful of all mediaeval popes and although he only held office from 1198 to 1216, his pontificate established a temporal and spiritual supremacy for the Holy See that was never fully surpassed under any other Pope.

Born Lotario de'Conti de Segni at Agnagni, he became the leading church lawyer of his time. Although he was not even a priest, and only 37 years old at the time of the death of Pope Celestine III, he was unanimously elected as Pope by the assembled cardinals and hurriedly ordained so he could assume the high office.

The judgment of the cardinals was soon vindicated as the new Pope set about introducing fundamental reforms of the church and enhancing the position of the Papacy in dealing with the rulers of Catholic kingdoms. He rapidly expanded direct Papal control over wide areas of Italy and Sicily and began to wield considerable authority over countries as widespread as Norway, Hungary and Poland.

He expanded and stabilised the international judicial network set up by his predecessors and introduced some integrity into the system for the first time. He also established the right of the Pope alone to appoint bishops throughout Europe, ensuring that he alone had control over their dioceses.

The Pope declared and put into practice his belief that all kings held their crown by virtue of the "Grace of God and of the Pope". In more poetical terms, he proclaimed:

> Just as the moon derives its light from the sun and indeed is lower than it in quantity and quality, in position and in power, so too the royal power derives the splendour of its dignity from the pontifical authority.

Demonstrating the temporal power he came to wield, he was instrumental in deposing Emperor Otto IV of Germany, after earlier crowning Otto as Emperor in Rome. He placed England under a Papal Edict and even excommunicated King John, because John refused to recognise the Pope's appointment of Stephen Langton as Archbishop of Canterbury. King John ultimately submitted to the Pope's authority and allowed England and Ireland to be declared satellites of the Holy See.

Although he had no armies under his command, he deployed a religious, legal and bureaucratic power that expanded the influence of the Papacy to establish himself as one of the major power players in Europe.

In church matters, he was instrumental in promoting the spiritual movement that led to the successful founding of the Franciscan and Dominican religious orders. He wrote a number of highly regarded encyclicals, including his remarkable treatise on the The Misery of the Condition of Man.

Under his auspices, the famous Fourth Lateran Council was convened in 1215, introducing uniformity of belief across a wide range of theological and doctrinal issues. It was also at his instigation that the Fourth Crusade was successful in conquering Constantinople, destroying the power of his Eastern rivals.

The main reason he is included in our list of *Whatever it Takes* characters is his treatment of the Cathars in southern France, during what is recorded in history as the "Albigensian Crusade". Although they were avowedly Catholic, the Pope had condemned the Cathars as being in league with the Devil. They had transformed the accepted depiction of Satan as a mischievous spoiler into a far more sinister and corrupting force for evil. Their name derives from the Greek word katharos (purity) and they believed that the message of the New Testament had been corrupted by the Catholic hierarchy, by ignoring the "Bad God" in the world who tempts us with material obsessions. The Cathars were outspoken critics of the Church for accumulating immense wealth and they loudly condemned the Pope as the richest man in Europe, whose cardinals, bishops and even local priests lived in relative luxury.

"as the moon derives its light from the sun and indeed is lower than it . . . so too the royal power derives the splendour of its dignity from the pontifical authority" — Innocent III

Church authorities were concerned that the Cathars were beginning to dominate areas of Europe. In the Languedoc region of France, they were reported to outnumber the Catholics. The Pope and the King of France were determined to suppress them, not only because of their doctrinal differences, but also because they refused to adhere to the orthodox dogma and standards of the church hierarchy. Heretically, they believed in the equality of women, allowing women to be involved in religious ceremonies and administration.

When the Pope's legate at Toulouse was murdered in 1208, after ten years of negotiations had failed to persuade the Cathars to abandon their heretical beliefs, His Holiness ordered that they should either be converted or exterminated. Inquisitions were conducted and many inhabitants were massacred when extensive areas of Languedoc and Toulousain were laid waste.

The war would last nearly 40 years and heretical towns including Carcassone, Toulouse, Lastours, Saissac and Beziers would need to be besieged for the Church to prevail. The Papal forces were determined to terrify the heretics by adopting ruthless tactics at the beginning of the conflict, correctly concluding that if they made an example of the towns they attacked early in the campaign, other major centres would surrender without costly sieges.

The main Papal army under the command of Arnaud-Amaury, the Abbot of Citeaux, besieged Beziers on 22 July 1209. The Catholic residents were permitted to leave unharmed, but some of the loyal Catholics opted to stay with the Cathars. Under the abbot's orders, all the remaining residents, nearly 15,000 people, were killed.

When one of the Church's soldiers dared to question the orders, asking how he could distinguish Cathars from loyal Catholics, the abbot replied:

> Kill them all. For the Lord knoweth those that are his.

King Henry V

[1386? 1387?–1422]

Henry V was arguably England's greatest "warrior king" after all he achieved during a short life. In fact, he only fought in two pitched battles, the first, as a 16 year old in the army of his father, Henry IV, at the battle of Shrewsbury. The young prince was nearly killed by an arrow that penetrated his cheek and lodged within his skull for some time before it was skilfully and painfully removed by a surgeon. He is mostly remembered however for the second, when he led and fought in the English army at the battle of Agincourt, achieving a stunning victory against overwhelming odds after invading France.

As we will see, his success was due in part to what we would now call a ruthless war crime committed against French prisoners of war.

Although he reigned for only nine years after his coronation in April 1413, and spent more than five years out of England, Henry remains one of the outstanding figures of English history. He conquered almost the whole of France in his attempt to unite it, before his premature death from dysentery at age 35.

He was born in Monmouth Castle in Wales in either 1386 or 1387, during the reign of his cousin Richard II, when his grandfather John of Gaunt was the King's guardian. Although his father was exiled during Richard's reign, the King cared for the young Henry and he accompanied the King on Richard's expedition to Ireland.

When Richard's rule was overthrown, Henry's father returned from exile to be crowned King Henry IV. Although he disagreed with many of his father's policies, young Henry did not attempt to undermine his reign. However he was banished from the King's Council in 1411. There is probably some truth in Shakespeare's account that he led a riotous existence in youth, before his coronation on 9 April 1413 following his father's death.

Henry V was determined to unite his kingdom and rapidly set about subduing the Lollards who had defied his father. After decisive military action, he arranged the execution of 39 prominent Lollards including their leader, Sir John Oldcastle, in 1417. Although he spent much of his reign fighting in France, he nevertheless introduced important civic reforms in England. Amongst his significant achievements were:

- He regularly made himself available to receive and adjudicate on petitions from the public, applying a rule of law which was both just and expeditious.
- He moved away from the use of French that had prevailed in the court and government of England for over three hundred years since the Norman invasion, and introduced English.
- He was instrumental in securing much needed reforms to the church, using diplomacy to help overcome the damaging schism that had prevailed until 1417, which had at one stage produced three popes, each claiming to be head of the church.

Henry was a pious man with deeply held religious beliefs. He attended mass every day, even when campaigning. He was resolute in upholding the traditional values and position of the church, but he acted decisively in purging the church of those clergy who were abusing their position and undermining its moral authority.

He was also an avid reader, a musician and gifted composer, who mastered the complexity of polyphonic church music. He was a generous patron of the arts and religious orders and he used his wealth to aid the poor and the underprivileged.

Although a man of conscience, he appeared to practise a Latin aphorism his father used to quote: *Necessitas non habet legem*—"Necessity has no law". Always mindful of what his conscience dictated, he was prepared to override it when it was incompatible with his duty as an effective king and when it conflicted with the unity of the church and of the state, which he regarded as paramount.

However, he is chiefly remembered for victories over the French and there is no doubt that he was the dominant military leader of his era. It is incredible to think that the enormous cost of maintaining an army in French territory was initially funded in part by pawning the Crown Jewels, and borrowing massive sums from wealthy citizens, who were prepared to lend money to the King.

After crossing the Channel, Henry successfully applied siege tactics he had perfected in subduing the Welsh rebellion inspired by Owain Glyndwr and was soon in control of Normandy. Henry was able to take advantage of deep divisions within the French aristocracy and soon controlled much of northwestern France, but by the time he came to confront the French army, the French had united against the invader. Henry's army was short of food and weakened by dysentery.

At Agincourt on 25 October 1415, the vastly outnumbered English army inflicted a heavy defeat on the French. With muddy conditions

hampering the heavily armoured French cavalry, the devastating accuracy of the English longbows decimated the French forces. The English also copied the French idea of repelling cavalry charges by driving sharpened stakes into the ground in front of their massed archers.

Leading his army in battle, Henry was felled by a blow from a French mace, following which the sword of the Duke of Alencon cleft his helmet. He recovered from both assaults and continued to inspire his men with his bravery.

Many French knights were killed when their horses foundered in the mud. Many others were captured and were being guarded by the last of Henry's reserves. When Henry was warned of an imminent French counter attack against his exposed rear, he ordered his men to execute most of these prisoners, apparently because he needed their guards to join the battle and was afraid the unguarded knights might re-arm.

There are wide discrepancies in the estimates of the number slaughtered, but the total most often quoted is 2,200. A number of those summarily executed were locked in a farmhouse that was set alight. Henry's order to kill the imprisoned knights was in breach of all the principles of warfare at a time when notions of chivalry still prevailed. Their slaughter was all the more remarkable considering that they were elite members of the French nobility, who could have been ransomed for substantial sums once the battle was over. Only a few hundred of the more prominent prisoners, including the Duke of Orleans, the Duke of Bourbon and Charles of Artois, Count of Eu, were spared to be ransomed later. Henry's ruthless killing of the rest has largely been ignored in the euphoric celebration of a resounding victory.

"Necessitas non habet legem"— Henry IV to his son

After returning to England, Henry renewed his campaign the following year, when he laid siege to the wealthy city of Rouen. The starving defenders released 12,000 unarmed residents, including women and children, expecting that the besieging army would allow them through its lines. But Henry refused to give them safe passage and they eventually died of starvation outside the city walls before Rouen finally fell in January 1419.

Henry V's actions can be contrasted with those of Henry II of England, who marched on Toulouse in 1159, with an army that vastly outnumbered the opposing French force. Although King Louis VII of France could not match Henry II in the field, he travelled to Toulouse and was within the city walls when the English King began his siege. Although he could have taken the city, Henry was reminded of an oath he had sworn to defend the life and person of the French King. Because an attack on the city would have amounted to a betrayal of his oath, Henry meekly withdrew, preferring the immense loss of prestige that resulted, than to be judged as someone who broke his oath.

Over 250 years later, Henry V continued his campaign and entered

Paris in triumph with his new father-in-law in tow, after the French King had given the eldest of the French princesses to Henry in marriage. His success is particularly remarkable for being achieved on the soil of a country with three times the size and population of England.

Following his military successes, he secured the Treaty of Troyes in 1420. Had he lived longer, it may have resulted in an enduring peace; however while besieging the city of Meaux, the King contracted dysentery and died in the early hours of 31 August 1422, aged 35.

In what may have been an attempt to redeem his actions and his soul, in his last will he made generous bequests to the abbey of Saint-Denis near Paris, and provisions for churches in other major French cities, where some of his victims would have originated.

Describing himself as a sinful man, he provided for 20,000 masses to be celebrated during the year following his death, together with three masses per day at stipulated times to be performed in perpetuity at Westminster Abbey, where his body is buried.

His conscience may have ultimately got to him.

Sir Thomas More

[1478–1535]

Thomas More was probably born on 7 February 1478 in Milk Street, Cheapside, just 20 yards from the birthplace of his famous namesake, the other great martyr and saint of the city of London, Thomas Beckett. Although each man died as a result of falling out of favour with his king, Beckett was savagely murdered within the sacred precincts of Canterbury Cathedral, whereas More's fate came at the hands of an executioner. More died largely for refusing to accommodate his King Henry's desire to annul his first marriage and be appointed head of the Church in England.

Most of More's family and many contemporaries believed he was acting irrationally, even foolishly. But More believed he was adhering to his Catholic faith and the law, taking his stance as a matter of conscience, even though he was aware that it would almost certainly cost him his life.

His name is still anathematic to some Presbyterians, but in 1935 he was canonised by Pope Pius XI and today he is remembered as a saintly figure, whose martyrdom at the hands of Henry VIII adds to his reputation as a man of principle—who adhered to a virtuous, even austere way of life, enduring the discomfort of a hair shirt for most of his adult life. Although his education caused him to regard logic and reason as paramount, he placed his faith above them.

More's contemporary and friend, Erasmus of Rotterdam, described him when he was in his forties as a scholarly and devout Christian who had dedicated himself to the affairs of the state, while fulfilling the role of an upright and modest *pater familias*.

As a young man, More had contemplated entering the priesthood, but his sexual urges led him to abandon the idea. He became a good husband instead of a bad priest. He was an avid reader and loved music, and although good humoured, with a dry wit, he adhered to an unwavering faith that dominated his existence.

In Holbein's famous portrait, we see a sombre but vivacious personality, with an all-devouring intellect shining through his grey eyes. He was animated and lively, with a passionate commitment to his family and was always omnivorous in his reading. Beneath the bright exterior, lay a stern resolve that would not compromise on his central beliefs.

After a period at Oxford University, More followed his father into the legal profession and was soon prospering as a barrister in the Inns of Court in London. His public profile grew when he acted for some of the merchant guilds of the city. Soon he was elected to Parliament and thereafter gave himself increasingly to politics. He published a scholarly and lucid account of the life of Richard III and was soon dominating the parliamentary debates, at barely 26 years old. When Henry VIII ascended to the throne, More was prevailed upon to enter the young King's service as a counsellor and diplomat and rapidly became one of Henry's most valued advisers.

His most famous book, *Utopia*, depicts an imaginary kingdom with a system of public education, and advocates a freeing of the mind for all, so that even workers could enjoy "the felicity of life".

More was the first to suggest that punishment should fit the crime in place of the cruel and disproportionate punishments which were the norm in his day. "Simple theft is not so great an offence as to be punished with death." He points out that if the thief and the murderer are sure of the same penalty, the law is simply tempting the thief to secure his theft by murder. He also suggested that prevention was more effective in suppressing crime than punishment. "If you do not remedy the evils which produce thieves, the rigorous execution of justice in punishing thieves will be vain."

In More's imaginary "Nowhere Land", legislation is designed to ensure the welfare—social, industrial, intellectual and religious—of the whole community, with a focus on the poor and underprivileged. He advocated religious tolerance, although as we shall see, his enlightened attitude did not persist during the later attack on the Catholic faith by Martin Luther and his followers.

"lawful, necessary and well done" — *More on the burning of heretics*

More petitioned Parliament to secure reforms of oppressive procedures in the Church courts and abuses of clerical patronage, but Luther's campaign was directed not only at the abuses of the Papacy, but at the Papacy itself and Luther's beliefs started to gain popularity, not only on the Continent, but in England.

When the once powerful Cardinal Wolsey fell out of favour, More agreed to accept the position of Lord Chancellor offered by the King, even though Henry must have known More would not support his determination to divorce Catherine of Aragon, in order to marry Anne Boleyn.

Like his friend Erasmus, More believed the piety and wisdom of the classic past could be harnessed with reason to regenerate both knowledge and religion. But Luther's doctrines would sweep away such notions, with a new emphasis on dogma annihilating hopes of unity and tolerance.

Although it was always left to the secular courts to determine the appropriate punishment and carry it out, there is little doubt that More was enthusiastic in his support for the heretics of his day being burnt at the stake, and that he had at least some direct involvement in the pursuit and interrogation of many of those ultimately found guilty of heresy.

The first heretic burnt at the stake after More became Lord Chancellor was former Catholic priest Thomas Hitton, arrested only a month after More had issued a proclamation against heretics. Hitton was found with prohibited Lutheran texts sewn into concealed pockets in his coat. Brought before the Archbishop of Canterbury, he openly admitted his heretical views. The secular authorities consigned him to the flames at Maidstone—"straight from the short fire to fire everlasting," as More put it.

More wrote extensively in an attempt to undermine Lutheran beliefs, but words were not enough to stem the tide flowing from the mainland of Europe and More resolved to use his power in direct and forceful action against non-believers. In 1530 the King issued two proclamations drafted by More, in which his majesty condemned the "malicious and wicked sects of heretics and Lollards" and urged state authorities to "give their whole power and diligence" to destroying them.

Contemporary records attest to More's participation from 1530 onwards in the fate of fellow Christians who were burnt to death before large crowds of the faithful, including:

Richard Bayfield—a former Benedictine monk and book trader
John Tewkesbury—a London haberdasher and leather merchant
John Frith—an avowed Protestant priest
James Bainham—a barrister from the Middle Temple, and
Thomas Bilney—a Cambridge scholar.

In one of his many pamphlets, "Dialogue Concerning Heresies", More clarified his position, declaring that the burning of heretics was "lawful, necessary and well done".

Even those who avoided the flames suffered cruelly at the hands of the authorities if they were found in possession of banned books. They were frequently interrogated by More in the notorious Star Chamber and consigned to the Tower of London. In the course of their journey through the streets of London, those who had been condemned were forced to ride facing the horse's tail, with extracts of the prohibited texts pinned to their clothing, while the obliging citizens pelted them with rotten fruit and dung. Others like the wealthy merchant John Peyt were left to perish in the Tower.

More was a unique combination of ambition and penitence, success and spirituality, who never deviated from his core beliefs. Unlike the pagans executed by Charlemagne, the men who burnt at the stake when More was Lord Chancellor were Christians to a fault. Their heresies did not embrace beliefs that derived from outside the text of the bible, yet they were persecuted and killed for what they believed.

The obvious question is why a man who was prepared to sacrifice his own life because of his adherence to conscientiously held beliefs, was determined to take ruthless action against fellow Christians whose conscience embraced only a different interpretation of Christ's message?

Whilst we would accept that his victims were only following their consciences, More was convinced their beliefs would not only undermine the position of the Catholic Church, but also be the harbinger of such social unrest and disorder in England as was occurring in parts of the Continent. He likened them to the plague and thought that their heresies were an insidious disease attacking the very heart of the Christian faith.

He correctly predicted that an acceptance of the Lutheran values would undermine and eventually displace the unchallenged position of the church in Rome, and he was determined to use his considerable power and authority to root out heretics and send for punishment anyone involved in the propagation of the new contagion.

As Peter Ackroyd points out, More firmly believed that acceptance of Luther's arguments supporting the primacy of individual belief and conscience, would open the way to decline in accepted orthodoxies and established beliefs. More correctly predicted that a thousand years of tradition and cohesiveness would begin to erode as the rise of self began.

In fairness to More, it should be emphasised that burning heretics was not an uncommon occurrence in England. It is estimated that in the hundred years before More's chancellorship, close to thirty were burnt at the stake for their beliefs. After More's death, the treatment by Henry VIII, and his new enforcer Thomas Cromwell, of those who supported or openly sympathised with More's position was at least as brutal as anything More had inflicted.

After Luther first published his blistering attacks on the Church, Henry VIII had written such a powerful reply that he was awarded the title "Defender of the Faith" by Pope Leo X. However the King became increasingly obsessed with the dissolution of his marriage to Catherine of Aragon, so he could marry Anne Boleyn, and More refused to approve. The disintegration of the previously close relationship between More and his King was also attributable to the fact that the King began to distance himself from More's pursuit of the heretics, realising that some of their beliefs in the primacy of the Crown over the Church would assist him in his other great ambition to be appointed head of the Church in England in place of the Pope. Ackroyd wrote:

> More believed, with much justification, that the destruction of the old religion was being undertaken at the behest of an arrogant and impetuous king, together with councillors who hoped to benefit from the disorder; The "reformation" was being imposed therefore upon a nation that remained generally pious and devoted . . . More saw further than most of his contemporaries; once the community of the faithful, the living and dead, was broken by schism then the faith itself would be placed in severe peril.

More eventually found his position untenable and resigned as Chancellor on 16 May 1532, banishing himself to the political wilderness. He may have hoped he could withdraw from the conflict, but the power behind the throne was now wielded by Thomas Cromwell, who was set on destroying More so the reforms of Church and State would be accepted. One of the first steps taken by Cromwell's ally Thomas Audley who succeeded More as Lord Chancellor was to release some forty Lutherans from prison.

When Cromwell insisted that More sign the new Oath of Allegiance, recognising Henry as the head of both the Church and the State in England, More refused. Despite attempts by his wife, by Cromwell and many parliamentary colleagues to have him accede to the King's demands, More refused to bend. After being incarcerated in the Tower and having his property confiscated, a perfunctory trial was convened during which the Solicitor General Richard Rich almost certainly perjured himself to secure a conviction. More was promptly found guilty and beheaded on 6 July 1535.

On the day before his execution, he wrote from his cell in the Tower his last letter to his beloved daughter, Margaret Roper, which concludes: "Fare well my dear child and pray for me, and I shall for you and all your friends that we may merrily meet in heaven."

Before the axe fell, contemporary accounts describe More calmly removing from the block the beard he had grown whilst in custody, saying "This hath not offended the King."

In October 2000, Pope John Paul II declared More the patron saint of Catholic statesmen and politicians.

Tsar Peter the Great

[1672–1725]

When Maria, the wife of Tsar Alexis, died in March 1669, there was no clear heir to the Miloslavsky throne. She had given birth to 13 children, but only two sons outlived her, neither of whom appeared fit to rule.

However the Tsar wasted no time in marrying a new Tsaritsa, Natalya, who duly gave birth to a son Peter on 30 May 1672. Alexis died when Peter was only three and a half. Peter was ten when, after the death of his older half brother, he was appointed to share the throne with his feeble-minded half brother Ivan, under the regency of their manipulative sister Sophia.

In 1689, Peter succeeded in having Sophia arrested and confined to a convent. Then when Ivan died in 1696, he assumed sole rule. He had displayed enormous energy, even from a young age, and insisted upon being trained in all military matters, at the expense of his general education. By age 22, he had grown to a towering 6 foot 7 inches, and despite habitual bouts of heavy drinking, he began to wield absolute power in the vast country.

He embarked on an ambitious campaign to reform Russia completely, starting by modernising the army and then creating for the first time a Russian navy, after Russia captured the strategic fortress of Asov on the Black Sea from the Turks.

Peter began to suffer from debilitating nervous convulsions, probably epileptic in origin, affecting his left side. There were several occasions when he had to be shielded from public view as the attacks became more noticeable.

He travelled through Europe for nearly two years, absorbing all he could of Western shipbuilding methods, and even worked as a shipwright in Dutch and English yards. During his stay in London, the Tsar and his retinue wrecked the home of the diarist John Evelyn, but Peter still found time to pose for a memorable portrait by Sir Godfrey Kneller.

In Peter's absence, four regiments of the Streltsy revolted in an attempt to place his half-sister Sophia on the throne, compelling him to return home urgently in 1698. The rebellion was ruthlessly suppressed and more than a thousand of the rebels were subjected to abominable tortures before their public execution, their bodies left to rot on public display as a deterrent. Peter even insisted on witnessing the torture, before returning to his feasting and drinking companions.

Having restored order, he stepped up his attempts to modernise Russia by importing skilled workers from all over Europe and sending young Russians abroad to acquire all the latest skills as shipwrights, engineers and builders. He started new schools, promoted education, opened the first museum and arranged for textbooks to be translated. He brought the Orthodox Church under state control and took over many of the monasteries. He insisted on his court adopting European habits of dress and abolished the wearing of beards, over vehement opposition. He was so enamoured with the new ships designed for his navy that he worked in the shipyards himself, sharing the food and conditions of the other workers.

After obtaining a treaty with the Turks, Peter turned his attention to the Baltic coast, where, after promising to abide by Russia's treaty with the Swedes, he declared war against them in 1700 in an attempt to reclaim Russian territory. Although he was sick with fever and bedridden much of the time, his active presence on the campaigns increased the sorely tested morale of the Russian troops. Church bells from all over Russia had to be melted down to replace the cannons captured by the Swedes. Being forced to endure winter in Lithuania, the Swedish army was devastated, with over 3,000 freezing to death in one night outside Gadyach. After his Cossack forces deserted to the Swedes, Peter had their capital Baturin burnt to the ground, and 7,000 of its inhabitants perished.

"The Tsar pulls uphill alone with the strength of ten, but millions pull downhill." — Ivan Pososhkov

The war dragged on for nearly 20 years, but after early defeats at the hands of the bold, young Swedish King, Charles XII, Peter finally achieved a decisive victory at Poltava, securing for Russia a firm foothold in the Baltic as well as the new territories of Estonia, Livonia and part of Finland.

In 1703, he founded a new capital, St. Petersburg, at the mouth of the River Neva. Despite marshy conditions there, and outbreaks of malaria, scurvy and dysentery that killed thousands, he compelled the entire Russian court to transfer to his new creation. Temporarily named Leningrad under Communist rule, it survives as one of the most elegant cities in the world. But Peter's actions made him many enemies, particularly amongst the still powerful nobility, although any sign of revolt was ruthlessly suppressed, so few dared to challenge him.

Peter introduced long overdue reforms of the civil service and administrative levels of government and imposed a poll tax as well as new taxes on such items as horses, hats, firewood, leather boots and even drinking water. State monopolies were established on profitable articles and commodities including coffins and salt.

Peter's measures provoked rising discontent, and his contemporary Ivan Pososhkov wrote: "The Tsar pulls uphill alone with the strength of ten, but millions pull downhill." Peter created the Secret Office to deal with any act or word considered treasonous.

While still married to Anna Mons, Peter became infatuated with Catherine, the Lithuanian servant girl, who was the mistress of his friend and collaborator Menshikov. Very soon Catherine became Peter's mistress and eventually he married her in 1712. Catherine bore him 12 children and eventually succeeded him after his death. She was crowned Empress of Russia on 27 May 1724 and accompanied him on all his official visits.

His son Alexis from his first marriage joined a faction opposed to Peter and when Peter was informed, Alexis fled to Austria and eventually Italy. After he had reached Naples in July 1717, Alexis received a letter from his father:

> My son, your disobedience and the contempt you have shown for my orders are known to all the world. Neither my words nor my corrections have been able to bring you to follow my instructions and last of all, having deceived me when I bade you farewell and in defiance of oaths you have made, you have carried your disobedience to the highest pitch by your flight and by putting yourself like a traitor under foreign protection . . . If you submit to my will by obeying and if you return, I will love you better than ever. But if you refuse then I as your father, by virtue of the power I have received from God, give you my everlasting curse; and as your sovereign, I declare you traitor and I assure you I will find the means to use you as such.

Alexis did not obey and the Tsar insisted that he be forcibly returned to Russia and prosecuted for his part in the attempted overthrow. After compelling him to name everyone who had assisted him, Peter had them all arrested and either painfully executed or banished into exile. Alexis was tortured, but died in mysterious circumstances before his father had determined his ultimate fate.

By relentlessly suppressing any hint of dissent, Peter had managed to transform Russia for the first time into a modernised European power. He was even prepared to sacrifice his son and heir in order to preserve his vision of what Russia should become.

Peter's health began to fail, particularly after a severe infection of his urinary tract which caused him almost constant pain. He died on 28 January 1725, with Catherine at his side. His last words were:

> I hope God will forgive me my many sins, because of the good I have tried to do for my people.

Oliver Cromwell

[1599–1658]

Oliver Cromwell was a fervent and sincere Puritan whose moral values played an important part in forming his personality and ambitions. He had become increasingly opposed to the arrogant and ruthless behaviour of England's King Charles I, particularly the King's disdain for Parliament. After helping to form and train the New Model Army, Cromwell led it to spectacular victories over the Royalist forces, enabling him to assume ever wider powers after the capture of the King.

He was born in Huntingdon, where he attended the local Grammar School, before moving to the Sydney Sussex College in Cambridge. He studied law in London and was elected to Parliament as Member for Huntingdon.

At the outbreak of the Civil War in 1642, Cromwell raised and trained a troop of cavalry, "The Ironsides", whose exploits were decisive in the battles of Marston Moor and Gainsborough. He assumed command of the New Model Army, ruthlessly suppressed a Royalist insurrection in Wales and defeated the Scots at the Battle of Preston.

Having captured the King, Cromwell instructed his Solicitor General John Cooke to draw up the unheard of charge against the King that he was a "tyrant, traitor and murderer". But it was treasonous to plot against the monarch, and there was limited support for Cromwell's desire to have the King executed. Out of a total of 507 elected members of Parliament, many absented themselves from the chamber, 45 were arrested and 186 were barred from entering by an armed group commanded by Cromwell's supporter Colonel Pride, in order to exclude anyone suspected of being unsupportive of Cromwell's aims.

Out of the 135 commissioners carefully selected by the 70 members of the "Rump Parliament", who were permitted to enter the building, less than 80 attended during the trial and only 59 (including Cromwell himself) were ultimately prepared to sign the death warrant which sent the King to his beheading on 30 January 1649.

As Winston Churchill described it in *A History of the English-Speaking People*, "This was not only a killing of a king, but the killing of a king who at that time represented the will and the traditions of almost the whole British nation." Cromwell, according to Churchill, had not only destroyed Parliamentary government, but "was about to plunge England in a tyranny at once more irresistible and more petty than any seen before or since".

The prophetic words of Cromwell's Solicitor General John Cooke after the King's execution were to haunt Cromwell for all his remaining years:

> Have pronounced sentence not only against one tyrant but against tyranny itself. Therefore if any of them shall turn tyrant, or consent to set up any kind of tyranny by law, or suffer any unmerciful domineering over the consciences, persons and estates of the free people of this land, they have pronounced sentence against themselves.

The King's last act before he was beheaded was to hand to Doctor Juxon, the Bishop of London, his blue sash containing the gartered jewel of Saint George and the solid onyx diamond, the emblems of his office, to be preserved for his son the Prince of Wales, uttering the single word "Remember". Indeed they did remember because after Cromwell's death, when the monarchy was restored at the hands of the King's son, the others responsible for the death of the King were all executed in gruesome circumstances, including Cooke, Peters, Harrison and seven others of the leading group.

Cromwell officially abolished the kingly office on 17 March 1749, along with the Privy Council and the Prerogative Courts, replaced by a Council of State establishing him in a position more absolute and unassailable than any monarch's. The House of Lords was abolished and many prominent peers including Lords Hamilton and Holland were executed. Cromwell even nominated his son as his successor, as kings had always done.

Cromwell then turned his attention to Ireland, where his army besieged Drogheda resulting in the massacre of almost 3,500 Royalist soldiers along with many civilians including every priest and friar, even after they had surrendered. A similar outcome followed the siege of Wexford, where Cromwell failed to prevent his troops from slaughtering the defenders and civilians. In a letter to Bradshaw after the campaign, he boasted, "It has pleased God to bless our endeavours at Drogheda . . . I believe we put to the sword the whole number of the defenders."

Although there had been earlier atrocities in Ireland, the slaughter at Drogheda and Wexford escalated the endless cycle of violence between the Catholic majority and the Protestant minority. Thousands of Irish men were banished as indentured slaves to the West Indies and many thousands more died of famine. Cromwell's legacy continued to haunt Ireland for decades and lasted well into the 20th century.

Despite the fact that the members of the Rump Parliament had been almost hand picked, Cromwell became frustrated with them also and on 20 April 1653, he again summoned his musketeers to the Parliament building and emptied the House of all remaining members, uttering the memorable words: "You have sat too long here for any good you have been doing. Depart, I say and let us have done with you. In the name of God go."

He thus abolished the last vestiges of a legally representative government, replacing it with an appointed body of Puritan notables, before that also fell out of favour and Cromwell assumed the title of Lord Protector in 1653. He then appointed 11 major-generals each to supervise the government of a province. He introduced laws banning gambling and penalising swearing, making adultery punishable by death and closing alehouses across the country. He banned celebrations of the mass and threw hundreds of Quakers into prison.

He repressed public debate, imposing strict controls over the press. All periodicals other than the two state-run newspapers were suppressed. At the same time those closest to the Lord Protector were able to enrich themselves with vast landed estates making the government and those controlling more hated than any regime in England before or since.

As John Drury described the situation the new Commonwealth had been transformed into a regime where Cromwell "alone holds the direction of political and military affairs in his hands. He is ONE equivalent to all, and, in effect King."

"if any of them shall turn tyrant, or consent to set up any kind of tyranny by law . . . they have pronounced sentence against themselves" —John Cooke

Cromwell was nevertheless as effective in his administrative reforms as he had been in leading his army. His ordinances curbed widespread corrupt practices. He swept away many barbarous punishments and provided relief for debtors. He found biblical justification for most of his actions and sincerely believed, as Napoleon would, that government could only be effective under an absolute ruler. He reorganised the Church of England consistent with his Puritan beliefs and introduced some religious tolerance, except for Catholics and Quakers.

He also enjoyed some success in the area of foreign policy, ending the wars with Portugal in 1653 and Holland in 1654. He made a Treaty with Catholic France which enabled him to defeat the Spanish at the Battle of the Dunes in 1658.

For some, Cromwell remains a defender of liberties and principle, who was instrumental in overthrowing a tyrannical king. If Cromwell had been prepared to work with a properly constituted Parliament after assuming power, it is likely that history would have treated him more favourably, because of the reforms he managed to introduce. However, he had no hesitation in imprisoning political opponents, and ultimately assumed and ruthlessly wielded absolute power after effecting the King's execution. Cromwell became an even greater tyrant than the monarch he replaced. His legacy did not survive the restoration that removed his son and brought King Charles II to the throne.

After Cromwell died on 3 September 1658, he was succeeded by his incompetent and inexperienced son Richard. It was hardly surprising that within two years, the late King's elder son was restored to the throne by popular acclaim. Many of those responsible for his father's execution suffered the same fate. Cromwell's body was disinterred from Westminster Abbey and hung from the gallows at Tyburn for all to see.

Although some historians still celebrate Cromwell as the heroic republican who was instrumental in bringing down an oppressive monarchy, the facts of his life demonstrate that despite his impressive military and administrative achievements, he only replaced one form of tyranny with his own equally ruthless and even more intolerant version.

Napoleon Bonaparte

[1769–1821]

Although he is still venerated in France, Napoleon must be remembered as a leader who practised the principles of Machiavelli—as he admitted in a letter to his brother Louis, after he had installed Louis as King of Holland "A prince who gets a reputation for good nature in the first year of his reign, is laughed at in the second."

Napoleon was born at Ajaccio on the island of Corsica in 1769. Soon after joining the French army he rose through the ranks of the republican forces after the overthrow of the French monarchy. But he was struck off the army list for returning late to his regiment in 1792, and later was charged with conspiracy, and briefly imprisoned, because of his friendship with the younger Robespierre who had made him a Brigadier General after his valuable performance in the siege of Toulon. Despite these career setbacks, he was appointed Commander of the Army in Italy in 1796 and soon his victories displayed his military genius.

After the French Revolution destroyed the old monarchy in 1789, thousands were executed by guillotine during the Reign of Terror, including the King himself and his queen Marie Antoinette. The increasing levels of lawlessness and anarchy which followed led to a coup installing Napoleon as First Consul in 1799.

Napoleon's continuing military successes and commendable administrative reforms enabled him to assume absolute power. He arranged for close rivals including Moreau and the Duke d'Enghien to be executed. One of his most outrageous acts to secure power for himself involved the kidnapping of the influential and aristocratic Louis de Bourbon-Conde, who was executed by firing squad on 21 March 1804. Charles-Maurice de Talleyrand-Perigord was the great survivor of French politics during every change of government. Despite his complicity in the murder he accurately remarked "It was more than a crime, it was a blunder."

Frustrated by the domination of the English navy in the Channel, Napoleon embarked on an expedition to Egypt and captured Malta, before arriving in Alexandria on 30 June 1798. But following the destruction of the French fleet at the hands of Admiral Nelson at the Battle of the Nile, he was eventually compelled to return to France in 1799.

Upon his return, he succeeded in having himself appointed as First Consul for ten years under a new Constitution and promptly founded the Bank of France to stabilise the franc and revive the moribund economy. He also embarked upon reforms of the judicial system and local government, which had both become very lax. He introduced an honour, the *Legion d'Honneur*, to reward acts of bravery, and improved the system of secondary education. France's network of roads and bridges was greatly improved and ports were rebuilt.

In 1801, he arranged for many of the prominent members of the Tribunate to be removed and replaced with his nominees. He divided it into three sections before having a measure passed that required it to deliberate *in camera* on laws and articles of the Civil Code, so that no dissent could be heard.

Within a few months of the Peace of Amiens being signed on 25 March 1802, the Republic began to be transformed into a system of government more like the monarchy it had replaced, including approval of Napoleon's right to appoint his own successor.

In 1804 he introduced the *Code Napoleon*, which unified and consolidated French law. It came to be adopted in wide areas of Europe under French control. Although it has been extensively revised it remains the core of many continental legal systems.

In 1808 Napoleon introduced the merit-based public exam, the Baccalaureate, which is still recognised worldwide. The new Imperial Catechism issued by government decree exhorted Catholics to pay their taxes and accept conscription. The Church was directed to teach its children that "To honour and serve our Emperor is thus to honour and serve God himself . . . We are forbidden to be disobedient to our superiors, to injure them, or to speak ill of them."

Napoleon has been described as having became "stupefied with his own omnipotence and infatuated with his own omniscience". Opponents were banished to asylums or committed to prison without trial by a system where the law condemned citizens on the strength of suspicion.

The harsh reality of life under Napoleon's tight grip is illustrated by the words of a general who addressed his troops at the time of the referendum to decide whether Napoleon should be installed as Consul for life: "You are free to hold your own opinion; nevertheless I must warn you that the first man not to vote for the consulate for life will be shot in front of the regiment." Napoleon was duly made First Consul for life and after the collapse of the Treaty of Amiens made preparations for an invasion of England.

Although Napoleon's success owed much to his early enthusiasm for republican principles, his increasingly dictatorial methods were accompanied by a return to all the trappings of royalty and subservient representatives of the *Ancien Régime* were appointed to key positions of power.

Napoleon's royalist tendencies peaked in 1804 when he coerced Pope Pius VII to come to Paris so he could be crowned as Emperor in Notre Dame Cathedral on 2 December 1804. In a gesture intended to assert his own authority and humiliate the Pope, Napoleon took the crown from the altar and placed it on his own head.

He also bestowed princely titles on family members and had himself crowned King of Italy in 1805. He made his brother Louis the King of

Holland and created the Confederation of The Rhine for his brother Jerome. His other brother Joseph was crowned King of Naples.

Many of his most ardent supporters became disillusioned with his betrayal of the republican cause. Beethoven, who intended to dedicate his superlative "Eroica" symphony to Napoleon was so disgusted by the news that Napoleon had been crowned Emperor that he tore up the dedication page in a rage, saying prophetically "Now he will also trample all human rights underfoot and only pander to his ambition; he will place himself above everyone else and become a tyrant."

One of Napoleon's enemies was the General Jean Baptiste Bernadotte who ultimately married Napoleon's former fiancée Desirée Clary. Desirée had earlier inspired Napoleon to write a romantic novella in her honour, *Clisson et Eugenie*, before he abandoned her in favour of Josephine. Desirée ultimately became Queen of Norway and Sweden when her husband became King at Napoleon's behest, largely to infuriate the English. After she had married, she perceptively described her former fiancée as "no longer concerned about France, but only himself, the Emperor. Instead he applied the Rights of Man to his own devices, paying lip service to freedom, while he enslaved the nation."

"If you see me master of France: well, I would not undertake to govern her for three months with liberty of the press." — Napoleon

---

After divorcing Josephine, Napoleon married Marie Louise, the daughter of the Emperor of Austria.

Despite successes against the Italians, the Austrians and the Russians, his forces were decisively beaten by the Duke of Wellington in Portugal, after the protracted Peninsular War. Worse for the French, after invading Russia in 1812 and occupying a deserted Moscow, Napoleon's Grand Armée was decimated by the Russian winter, and only a small fraction of the enormous invading force made it back to French territory.

Although he had further military successes, he was forced to abdicate when the allies attacked Paris. He was banished to Elba, but made a heroic return to France after Louis XVIII had been restored to the throne, re-entering Paris after the King fled. During the "Hundred Days" he became Emperor again. But confronted at Waterloo by combined armies of Prussia under Blucher and England under Wellington, Napoleon was decisively defeated on 18 June 1815. He was banished to the remote island of St. Helena where he died on 5

May 1821. The circumstances of his death remain controversial: he may have been poisoned, but more likely died from liver disease and cancer.

It is now estimated that 2.5 to 3.5 million men were killed in the military conflicts of the Napoleonic wars, but the civilian deaths were probably even higher. Napoleon's forces committed massacres against minorities in different parts of Europe, especially the insurgents in Spain. Recent research has revealed that Napoleon's troops resorted to using gas against civilian populations in Haiti.

Ambition transformed Napoleon from being a hero of liberty to one of the most ruthless of military tyrants. He frankly admitted his undermining of the Constitution when addressing the Conseil d'Etat: "Every day brings the necessity to violate constitutional laws; it is the only way, otherwise progress would be impossible."

He positively hated lawyers and was quoted as saying "I should like to cut out the tongues of barristers who use them against the government." He had earlier decreed that 50 out of 63 newspapers in Paris be suppressed and that every book currently for sale be submitted to a Commission of Revision for scrutiny.

As he admitted in a letter to the Austrian Foreign Minister, Prince Metternich, "If you see me master of France: well, I would not undertake to govern her for three months with liberty of the press."

Even more illustrative of his authoritarianism was his statement: "There is only one secret of managing the world and that is to be strong, because in strength there is no error or illusion; that is the naked truth." As he said to Jean-Antoine Chaptal: "Both within and without, I only reign by the fear I inspire."

Apart from military tactics, Napoleon was generally disdainful of any study of history, describing it as: "a fairy tale told by the victors". He even banned the Roman historian Tacitus because "the analysis of the motives of tyrants would lead to dangerous comparisons." The great French writer Madame de Stael was compelled to spend much of her life in exile, prompting her to say that France had become "a garrison where military discipline and boredom rule."

He was probably the outstanding military tactician of history as commander of fanatically loyal troops, and few would contest his success as a civil administrator. His legal codes and centralised administrative systems have endured to this day in France and other countries of Europe. However he was ambitious primarily for himself, unscrupulous and frequently ruthless.

As with all historical figures, extreme caution should of course be exercised in judging the actions of both Cromwell and Napoleon by today's standards. Certainly neither matches the even more notorious and ruthless dictators of the 20th century. It must also be conceded that they were both men of exceptional talent especially in their military and administrative achievements. Nevertheless, they should not be venerated, as both were prepared to use their power to suppress opposing views ruthlessly, in ways even more intolerant than the oppressive regimes they helped overthrow.

There is little doubt that freedoms of speech and association were ultimately more undermined than enhanced during the reign of both men and their exploits remind us that just because there are perceived injustices and faults in a system, does not mean it should be wholly discarded, at least until we have a clear idea what is proposed as a suitable replacement.

Admiral Horatio Nelson

[1758–1805]

Horatio Nelson is venerated as the hero of the Battle of Trafalgar in October 1805, when his comprehensive defeat of the French Fleet saved Britain from an invasion by Napoleon, but during his career, his reckless disobeying of orders from his superiors could well have had disastrous consequences. Earlier in 1805, a French Fleet commanded by Admiral Villeneuve escaped from Toulon harbour, leading Nelson in pursuit all the way to the Antilles, leaving the English navy weakened and exposed if the French had been astute enough to take advantage of the situation.

Nelson was born on 29 September 1758, the son of the local pastor. After a basic education, he was allowed to join his uncle aboard the *Raisonnable* in the Royal Navy when only 12 years of age. He rose rapidly through the ranks to command his first ship in his early 20s. He suffered from acute sea sickness all his life and sustained a near fatal bout of malaria while serving in India, leaving him with a recurrent partial paralysis. In the course of active duty he repeatedly exposed himself to danger, and suffered serious wounds. Later he wrote "I know it is in my disposition that difficulties and dangers do but increase my desire of attempting them."

While serving in the West Indies Nelson met and married his wife, the widowed Mrs. Nisbet and also befriended Prince William, the Duke of Clarence. Like many men of action, Nelson found life tedious in times of peace and tended to become more overbearing. His persistent disregard for authority and intemperate letter writing on inconsequential matters did not endear him to those above him and his career languished from 1787 after he returned from the West Indies—until January 1793, a few weeks before war was declared with France, when he was finally given a command: the *Agamemnon*.

He captured the towns of Bastia and Calvi on the island of Corsica, losing his right eye in the Calvi engagement. In a disastrous attempt to capture Tenerife, the injury he sustained to his right arm, necessitated its amputation. He nevertheless distinguished himself at the Battle of St. Vincent against the Spanish fleet, resulting in him being appointed a rear admiral in 1797.

After a lengthy pursuit, Nelson surprised a fleet of 13 French ships in the Nile Delta and achieved an overwhelming victory, in the course of which he sustained a serious head injury, as well as a return of his malarial symptoms and extreme fever.

During an earlier stay in Naples, he had become enamoured with Emma Hamilton, the beautiful young wife of the British envoy, Sir William Hamilton, and their tempestuous and scandalous relationship was to endure for the rest of his life. He achieved worldwide fame after his victory in the Battle of the Nile, and sailed his battered ship and body back to Naples into the enthusiastic and accommodating arms of Lady Hamilton, who had written to him: "I walk and tread in air with pride, feeling I was born in the same land with the victor Nelson and his gallant band."

Although almost certainly aware of his wife's enthusiasm for the hero of the moment, Lord Hamilton offered Nelson accommodation at his Palazzo Sessa, assuring Nelson that "Emma is looking out for the softest pillows to repose the few wearied limbs you have left." Nelson had no hesitation in accepting the offer and settled into a life of luxury at the Palazzo to complete his recuperation, all naval ambitions deferred.

When Naples was under threat from forces sympathetic to the French, Nelson assisted the King of Naples and his court to evacuate to Sicily, where they remained for some time before Royalist forces under the command of Cardinal Ruffo succeeded in reclaiming the city from the Jacobites. Nelson returned to Naples with three British ships of the line and proceeded to assert his authority over the city in complete disregard for the terms of the peace treaty which Cardinal Ruffo had negotiated with the French and their Neapolitan allies.

Although he had no orders, nor any authority to execute anyone, Nelson arranged for the summary trial and hanging of anyone suspected of having collaborated with the Jacobites during the short period of their occupation of the city. Prominent members of the aristocracy were amongst those hung from the yardarms of the British warships, including some of the best looking women in Naples, despite pleas for mercy on their behalf from the Queen herself.

Francesco Caracciolo was amongst the first to be executed as a former commander of the Neapolitan navy, followed shortly afterwards by many other prominent Neapolitans, including Dr Domenico Crillo, a leading professor of botany who had served as court physician and was close to the Queen. Nelson had convinced himself that an example needed to be made of those who had co-operated with the cause of the French and he was ruthless in pursuing them and arranging their execution. As far as he was concerned, it was simply a case of putting into practice his fervent belief: "You must consider every man your enemy who speaks ill of your king and . . . you must hate a Frenchman as you hate the devil."

His actions were even more extraordinary, when it is recognised that under the terms of the treaty signed by the Cardinal, the French were guaranteed safe passage back to France and that in addition to those he had executed, there were hundreds who perished in the atrocious conditions aboard the *polaccas* stranded in the harbour, waiting in vain for permission to leave for France, in accordance with the treaty.

Nelson's continued presence in Naples to be with his beloved Emma was in breach of express orders he had received from his superiors to secure Minorca. As he frankly admitted to Lord Spencer: "I am prepared for any fate which may await my disobedience."

The extent to which Nelson had sacrificed his duty to be with Lady Emma is well illustrated by the remark made by his exasperated Commander-in-Chief Lord Keith: "Lady Hamilton has had command of the fleet long enough."

Nevertheless the King of Naples, upon his return, endorsed the actions Nelson had taken and rewarded him with a 30,000 acre estate on the slopes of Mt. Etna in Sicily, as well as bestowing on him the title of Duke of Bronte.

After a lengthy overland journey with his pregnant mistress, Nelson finally returned to England on 6 November 1800, to a less than enthusiastic reception from the Lords of Admiralty and his long-suffering wife, leaving her with little choice but to accept the situation. However by the public at large he was feted as a hero wherever he went. His already considerable vanity was inflated by the welcome he received during an extensive journey he made across the country.

His acrimonious relationship with his superiors was exacerbated by a long running dispute with his commander, the Earl of St Vincent—who said of Nelson: "He is vain and weak and therefore open to flattery and all its concomitants." Nelson ultimately succeeded in litigation he instituted against the Earl, the court ruling that Nelson was entitled to resist the Earl's demand for a share of the prize money captured by the fleet, when he was absent overseas at the time of the battle.

Although there were numerous prizes he had seized during his career, frequently leading the boarding party in storming the enemy ship, Nelson never profited greatly from ships he captured. "True Honour, I hope predominates in my mind, far above riches." He never achieved great wealth, largely because he was always generous not only to his wider family, but to former comrades in arms and friends.

Despite the continuing scandal, his affair with Emma Hamilton persisted even after their return and she gave birth to their illegitimate daughter Horatia on 29 January 1801. Even after returning to active duty, Nelson continued to write up to four letters a day to Emma, repeatedly expressing his undying love.

At the Battle of Copenhagen later in 1801, Nelson was able to achieve a resounding victory over the Danish defenders of the city, leading to the treaty which produced a peaceful resolution of the Baltic crisis. Typically however, his success was only achieved after he deliberately put his telescope to his blind eye, in order to ignore signal flags ordering him to withdraw, hoisted by the commander of the fleet, Sir Hyde Parker. He said "I have only one eye—I have a right to be blind sometimes . . . I really do not see the signal." He thus achieved one of his great successes by again deliberately ignoring the order of a commanding officer. This time however, it was his timid superior, Sir Hyde Parker, who was recalled, and Nelson was appointed Commander-in-Chief, until relieved by Admiral Pole.

Partly because of the highly publicised scandal of his personal life and also his thinly disguised contempt for incompetent superiors, Nelson spent many years out of favour with the Lords of Admiralty, despite his outstanding successes as a commander. On the day Lord Hamilton died, war was again declared on France and when a French invasion again loomed as a real possibility, it was Nelson who was summoned for duty and placed in charge of the fleet. His tactics were instrumental in engaging and defeating the combined French and Spanish fleets off Cape Trafalgar on 21 October 1805.

However, he was mortally wounded by a sniper's bullet and after being informed that an overwhelming victory had been achieved with the destruction or capture of 18 enemy ships and no British ships lost, he died aboard his ship *HMS Victory* about three hours later. His last words were "Thank God, I have done my duty."

"You must consider every man your enemy who speaks ill of your king . . . you must hate a Frenchman as you hate the devil." — Nelson

---

His body was placed in a cask of brandy mixed with camphor and myrrh and transported back to England along with the news of the battle which saved England from invasion. The glory of his victory and the circumstances of his death caused all his faults to be forgotten. As Machiavelli had earlier written in *The Art of War*, "A battle that you win, cancels any other bad action of yours."

Nelson had overcome many handicaps and tribulations in achieving his outstanding successes. Apart from his *Whatever it Takes* moment in Naples, he was not cruel nor as ruthless as many of the characters we have encountered, but his determination and confidence enabled him to fulfil his ambitions, even in the face of significant physical problems and entrenched opposition.

His life was replete with paradoxes and contradictions, because although he was a strict disciplinarian with those he commanded, he ignored orders from above when he judged it convenient to do so. He was a dedicated patriot who fearlessly pursued the ships of those who threatened England, yet during his time in Naples, his infatuation with Lady Hamilton, caused him to be completely derelict in his duty as a serving naval officer, much to the exasperation of his superiors.

He was a man of high moral standards, yet he flaunted his affair with Emma, knowing only too well that in the eyes of many, it was completely unacceptable for two married people to conduct such a relationship in public.

However, it is fair to conclude that in all other respects, he displayed throughout his life what he called "conscious rectitude". His short autobiography sums up his life in suitably understated and modest terms:

> Thus may be exemplified by my life, that perseverance in any profession will most probably meet its reward . . . And may I say to the Reader, "Go thou and Do likewise."

Themistocles

[523–458 BC]

Our next character was also a naval hero, 2,300 years earlier during the era of Classical Greece, when Athens and other city states were threatened by the overwhelming forces of the Persians under King Xerxes. Despite the heroic deeds of Leonidas and his 300 Spartans, who all died fighting myriads of Persians at Thermopylae in 480BC, the Persians overran much of Greece. Only the Greek naval forces were undefeated. It was largely because of the genius of the Athenian, Themistocles, that Greece and what became the foundation of Western civilisation was saved.

Much like Nelson, Themistocles did not resort to violent or cruel measures, but he was capable of deliberate deceit and ruthless cunning and used his manipulative skills to great effect against friend and foe, in order to overcome or marginalise those who opposed him. On the scale of reprehensible behaviour, despite his ruthless ambition, he is included as only a very minor offender, mainly because he never hesitated to resort to any level of deception and intrigue to win the day.

Born in 524BC, Themistocles, who came from humble origins, grew up in Cynosarges, the immigrant area of ancient Athens, and his mother may have been a prostitute. But his talents were recognised even at a young age, when one of his teachers said "My boy, you will be nothing insignificant, but definitely something great, either for good or evil."

His early life was dissolute and degenerate being sufficiently wayward for his father to disinherit him. However, after participating in the epic victory over the Persians at Marathon, he was inspired by Mnesiphilus to dedicate himself to public life, saying "The wildest colts become the best horses, when they receive proper training and discipline."

He rose rapidly to a position of influence as the newly created democratic system of government, championed by Cleisthenes, gradually took hold in Athens. By appealing to the masses he was elected Archon in 492BC. He prided himself on never forgetting a voter's name and developed his oratorical skills in his practice as an attorney and mediator.

It was expected that having obtained popularity and influence, he would agree to a proposal that the stream of money flowing from a new silver deposit discovered at Laurium, close to his home town, would be

distributed by a payment of 10 drachma to every citizen. However, Themistocles surprised many by opposing the idea.

Being acutely mindful of the threat posed by the Persian Empire, Themistocles convinced his fellow Athenians to apply the money for a greatly expanded navy only as a result of lying to them about the threat to their trade ambitions supposedly posed by the nearby island of Aegina. He recognised that there was an entrenched group in Athens who were committed to appeasing the aggressors from the East and it was only as a result of his ruse and the power of his oratory that Themistocles managed to persuade the Assembly to invest in a large new fleet of three-tiered galley triremes. His success was all the more remarkable because he achieved it over the vehement opposition of his main rival Aristides.

He realised that the power of Athens and its very survival depended upon it having a dominant fleet and he was also instrumental in consolidating and fortifying the three natural harbours at Piraeus, giving Athens protected access to the sea.

When the Persians invaded Greece under their King Xerxes in 480BC, with an army probably in excess of 200,000 men and a supporting fleet of more than 1,000 ships, they vastly outnumbered the combined forces of the Greek states.

Two actions taken by Themistocles at the height of the crisis illustrate just how unscrupulous and greedy he was. Herodotus tells us that he accepted 30 talents from the Euboeans to persuade the Athenians not to abandon their island. He duly passed on 8 talents of the monies paid in support of the cause but kept the rest for himself.

As the invasion drew closer to Athens, a corrupt demagogue called Epicydes decided to nominate for the position of general and it was widely expected that he would be successful. Themistocles took it upon himself to pay Epicydes a generous bribe, in return for his withdrawal from the contest.

The Greeks consulted the Oracle at Delphi, who advised the Athenians to abandon their city, saying: "The wooden wall alone remains unassailable."

As was so often the case, the Oracle was ambiguous, because in those days the Acropolis of Athens was surrounded by a wooden rampart. Those reluctant to abandon the city argued that it was those wooden ramparts to which the prophetess was referring. It was Themistocles whose oratory once again persuaded the Athenians that the message referred to the wooden ships of the Athenian navy. He convinced them to abandon the city, evacuating the women and children to safety at Troezen in the Peloponnesus, and committing every able-bodied man to operate the three banks of oars aboard the triremes.

As a result of Themistocles' earlier efforts, Athens had the biggest contingent of triremes of all the Greek cities and although Eurybiades of Sparta had overall command, it was Themistocles who dictated the tactics the Greek navies adopted. Themistocles correctly concluded that the only chance of victory for the hugely outnumbered Greeks rested in luring the Persian fleet into the narrow strait separating the island of Salamis from the mainland. When some of the Greek commanders threatened to withdraw their ships, Themistocles used flattery and diplomacy to persuade them to stay. At the same time he sent his trusted servant Sicinnus to the Persian commander, telling him the Greeks were fighting amongst themselves, that Themistocles and the Athenian navy would desert to the Persians once the fleets were engaged, and that the Persian fleet should manoeuvre to trap the Greek ships in the Strait.

The ruse worked to protect any Greeks from retreating. The Persians advanced into the strait the next morning under the confident gaze of Xerxes, who had installed his throne on the mainland to watch the battle unfold. The confined waters hampered the deployment of the more numerous but less manoeuvrable Persian vessels, where they were confronted by the well trained and prepared Greek ships. Themistocles also held back from engaging the enemy vessels until the reliable strong winds had arrived, causing the higher Persian ships to become unstable. The tactics were spectacularly successful and the navy secured a great victory.

Although Themistocles urged that the fleeing Persians be pursued and their bridge to Asia across the Hellespont be destroyed to trap them in Europe, he was overruled by Eurybiades, who decided that the Persians should not be impeded in retreating completely from Greek territory. Deviously, Themistocles sent a secret messenger to the Persian King falsely claiming that it was his personal intervention that saved the Persians from being pursued. It was a complete fabrication that was to prove very helpful to Themistocles later in his life.

Flushed with his military success, Themistocles proposed to the Assembly that Athens should destroy the beached ships of the other Greek city states to ensure the future superiority of the Athenians, but his proposal was defeated. He did embark upon fortifying the city with long walls that connected it to the naval base at Piraeus. After initially assuring the Spartans that no such work was being carried out, he then invited their ambassadors to inspect the work once it was capable of being defended. Understandably, the Spartans never forgave him.

He also embarked on a campaign to brutally punish and extract heavy monetary penalties from islands which had assisted the Persians, even besieging the island of Andros. Such tactics made him very unpopular amongst many members of the Delian League, which had just been formed under Athenian leadership, ostensibly to continue the struggle against Persia.

Although the primacy of his position in Athens gradually declined, Themistocles continued to play an important role in Greece, by opposing Sparta and actively encouraging democratic reforms in Arcadia and Argos. His opposition to Sparta was perceived as undermining the unity of the Greek states. Later events were to prove that he was right in not trusting the military ambitions of the Spartans, once the Persian threat had faded.

He was ultimately brought down by the influence of the Spartans and enemies from within who resented the power he had come to wield. He was ostracised by Athens and eventually charged with assisting the Persians. He went first to Argos but he was then pursued from one refuge to another and eventually arrived in Asia Minor where he spent time in Ephesus and entered the Persian Empire.

Themistocles obtained an audience with Xerxes' son, Artaxerxes, who had succeeded to his father's throne and reminded Artaxerxes of his earlier intervention in supposedly saving the Persians from being pursued. The new King was obviously impressed by their former adversary because he was well treated and granted the revenues of a number of cities including Lampsacus and Magnesia.

"The wildest colts become the best horses, when they receive proper training and discipline." — Themistocles

---

He never returned to Greece and died at age 65, in Magnesia, after drinking ox blood or poison. There are suggestions that he committed suicide rather than assist the Persians in a new campaign against the Greeks, but there is little surviving evidence. At the same time, there is no evidence that Themistocles ever betrayed the cause of the Greeks with the Persians. He seems to have found favour with his former enemies solely because of their respect for his abilities and wise counsel.

There are surviving copies of letters purportedly sent by Themistocles during his period of exile. Although much of their contents is of dubious authenticity, they contain powerful passages that provide a telling insight into the life of a man who appears as "a great though pathetic patriot, absolved from any guilt and driven to desperate actions because he had been betrayed by ruthless and vindictive men."

The letters bemoan his fate after his fall from grace as the hero of Salamis and repeatedly complain about how unfairly he has been treated by those who he helped to save. Understandably, they also express amazement at how well he has been treated by the Persian King, when he "never told or wrote to him anything that was true".

To his old rival Aristides, he wrote:

> For you were unjust to me, but he is ready to help me who was wronged; and you are the ones who made me pitiable by driving me out, but he rightly took pity upon me, the one who had been expelled.

He alone envisaged an enduring Athenian empire, based upon naval supremacy. When he was frustrated in that aim and worse, expelled from the city he loved, threatened with death by those who had always resented the power he wielded, he was driven to take refuge amongst former enemies who respected him, even though they opposed what the Greeks tried to uphold.

It was only after his death that the citizens of Athens remembered all that he had done for the city, and he is revered to this day as one of the great leaders of the Athenians. To achieve his aims, Themistocles had been prepared to grossly mislead his city, his allies and of course the enemy, pursing what he considered the best interests of the state. The fact that in many instances it also advanced his own power, and position and wealth, never impeded his determination. He was ruthless and arrogant but also charming and beguiling.

As his biographer, Robert Lenardon puts it, his life was an interesting combination of "duplicity, versatility and ingenuity", enabling him to inspire his countrymen at the time of their greatest crisis. There is little doubt that it was his words and actions that were decisive in saving his country and its Hellenic civilisation. Lenardon succinctly describes him as a man who was:

> A particular mix of virtue and vice, that made such an effective politician.

The Salem Witch Trials

[1692–93]

Although it is not possible to single out one individual to blame for the barbaric events that occurred in and around the village of Salem, Massachusetts, near Boston, the whole community can be condemned for failing to halt the hysterical persecution and execution of alleged witches that occurred there over 14 months.

Between February 1692 and May 1693 at least 19 people, including 14 women, were executed, and seven others died in prison. A 70 year old farmer, Giles Corey, died after three days beneath a crushing weight of stones, because he refused to plead to the allegation of witchcraft made against him. He was the only person in the history of America to suffer such a dreadful fate after two days of excruciating pain.

In January 1692, the young daughter and niece of the Reverend Samuel Parris both fell ill and began to suffer convulsive seizures, screaming obscenities and blaspheming. The local doctor, William Griggs could find no medical explanation and agreed with the family's conclusion that it was "the Devil's Influence".

On being closely questioned, the girls implicated three women in their behaviour, Sarah Good, Sarah Osborne and Tituba, the Indian slave in the Parris household. The three women were brought to trial and although the first two denied any involvement, sensationally Tituba admitted that "the devil came to me and bid me serve him." She provided a vivid description of having been visited by a tall white haired man in a serge coat as well as having seen a hog, a great black dog, a red cat, a black cat, a yellow bird and a hairy creature that walked on two legs.

She claimed to have signed a pact with the Devil in blood and implicated her two co-accused as being involved in the Devil's work. She insisted that many more were involved. Sarah Good was amongst the first committed to the gallows and Sarah Osborne died after nine weeks of imprisonment. Although Tituba herself spent time in jail, she survived and was one of those who eventually received a pardon when the madness finally subsided the following year.

By May 1692, at least eight Salem girls claimed to have been placed under the Devil's evil spell and the accusations of witchcraft began to spread to an ever-widening circle of witches and wizards that ultimately totalled approximately 185 people, unleashing an increasingly hysterical

conviction in the tightly knit community that the Devil was trying to undermine their Puritan faith and subvert the whole country. The accepted wisdom was that it was preferable to nominate someone as a witch before someone else mentioned your name.

Of the afflicted women, we are able to identify four who were married, three maids and three girls less than 12 years of age. Two 16 year old girls, Mary Walcott and Elizabeth Hubbard, made the greatest number of accusations closely followed by 14 year old Abigail Hobbs (who sent both her parents to prison) and 19 year old Mercy Lewis.

One of the first of the accused to hang was the church going grandmother Martha Corey, whose poignant plea was ignored when she said: "We must not believe all that these distracted children say."

Although the village itself had only 550 residents, accusations soon spread to neighbouring areas. The senior minister at nearby Andover, Dane Francis, discovered that he was related to 22 accused witches, with one in every 15 people being included amongst the accused. In the months that followed, more than a hundred witches were indicted, a quarter of them being men. Although some escaped from jail, most were found guilty and 19 were hanged.

Once unleashed, the accusatory atmosphere intensified with the fear that the village had been corrupted by those colluding with the Devil.

Prevailing food shortages were identified as evidence of God's punishment for what was occurring. Paranoia and underlying prejudices caused the community to turn on itself as people were condemned in many cases based only on spectral evidence, enabling individuals who had never met their accusers to be convicted of crimes that only existed in the imagination of others. Some were convicted on the strength of confessions that were only forthcoming after the accused had been tied by the neck and heels until blood emerged from the nose.

In fairness to the participants, it must be recognised that witch hunts had been widespread in Europe for hundreds of years with burning at the stake being the most common sentence imposed. Amongst avowedly Christian communities, a practice of singling out witches for torture and painful death had flourished from the time of the Inquisition. Church authorities instigated and perpetuated cruel practices in an attempt to root out the cause of evil in the community, but in doing so they had created a malevolent regime that generated a level of persecution that was worse than the world had ever before seen.

In 1515, there were 500 witches burnt at the stake in Geneva alone and in 1524, 1,000 executions were carried out in Como, Italy. In the hundred years prior to 1680, England, Scotland and Wales had executed nearly 4,000 witches. However, by 1682, following strident criticism of the witchcraft trials in England by the Lord Chief Justice Sir Francis North, the practice gradually began to decline, but by then it had been seamlessly transferred to the New World.

When the New England colonists established a Criminal Code in 1641, the first capital crime was idolatry and the second was witchcraft, with the code providing:

> If any man or woman be a witch, that is, has or consults with a familiar spirit, they shall be put to death.

With the legislation so loosely drafted, it is little wonder that the trials so frequently resulted in convictions particularly when the expectations of the local populace insisted that any evil influences must be expunged.

Going back to where it all started, one of the few books that was found in the library of the Reverend Parris, was *Memorable Providences, Relating to Witchcrafts and Possessions*, a controversial book by a Boston minister, Cotton Mather, which had been published in 1689 and widely reported. Mather dealt in lurid detail with the practices of witchcraft by an Irish Catholic washerwoman Goody Glover. We will never know whether the book had any role to play in starting the witch hunt that exploded in the small community, but it is likely that it played some part.

Mather attended and reported on many of the Salem trials and was present on 19 August 1692, when four men were executed on the same day. Amongst those who were hanged that day was a young farmer, John Proctor, who had been arrested along with his pregnant wife and the rest of his family, following his criticism of the accusers, whose spectral evidence was being relied on to secure the convictions. According to Proctor's petition, the only accusation made against him arose after a person accused of witchcraft had been tortured.

In 1691, A New England Charter had been issued by the King of England, which was perceived as an attempt to undermine the religious beliefs of the English colonies in the New England region which embraces Massachusetts. By all accounts, they may have been credulous and easily swayed but these were good people, who felt compelled to resort to extreme and malevolent measures to try to eliminate the evil they had convinced themselves existed.

If any man or woman be a witch, that is, has or consults with a familiar spirit, they shall be put to death. — Criminal Code, 1641

As Stacy Schiff points out in her recent book on the Salem witches: "When diabolical machinations are what you are watching for, they quickly became what you saw... Multiple inconsistencies and contradictions in the accounts provided by the bewitched were ignored as a product of the devil addling their brains."

Despite, and some would say partly because of, their deeply held religious beliefs, the community was prepared to condemn and sentence to death anyone who was suspected of being aligned with the forces of the Devil. Food shortages and unseasonal weather patterns only added fuel to the hysterical behaviour of the god fearing citizens.

The jails were soon overflowing with suspects and the newly appointed Governor, Sir William Phipps, appointed his Deputy Governor, Sir William Stoughton, to preside over the trials assisted by a panel of judges and empanelled juries. Despite his legal training and high reputation, Stoughton fell under the sway of the condemnatory atmosphere and allowed the accusers a free rein in recounting their diabolical visions of the accused. One of the few of the accused to be acquitted by a jury was 71 year old Rebecca Nurse. However Stoughton took it upon himself to substitute a guilty verdict. A pardon issued by the Governor was later reversed and Rebecca was executed along with four other women on 19 July 1692.

The first indication that the hysteria might be abating arose after 17 year old Margaret Jacobs announced on the eve of his execution, that she had invented all of her allegations against her grandfather. He was nevertheless executed along with three other men on 19 August 1692. History does not disclose whether it arose from writer's cramp or as a matter of principle, but the Andover Justice of the Peace, Dudley Bradstreet, refused to issue any new arrest warrants. No such qualms afflicted the Essex County Sherriff, George Corwin, who took full advantage of the arrests, to ransack the estates of the accused even before their convictions.

The extent to which the justice system failed is illustrated by the fact that, with the exception of Samuel Wardwell, all those who admitted their witchcraft were spared the gallows, but all who maintained their innocence and were duly found guilty were executed.

When the wife of Governor Phipps authorised the release of one suspect, her name was included amongst the accused. Partly to protect his wife and partly in an attempt to salvage his political fortunes, the Governor finally intervened in October 1692, when he postponed further prosecutions and ordered that the court be disbanded. Although the victims and the judgment of history would applaud his actions, the standing of Governor Phipps deteriorated, compelling him to travel to England, where he died in 1695, when he was replaced as Governor by the presiding judge, Sir William Stoughton.

The jails finally began to empty and the executions came to an end. Eventually a pardon issued for most of the victims along with the payment of some compensation to their families, but it was not till 2001 that the last of the condemned were finally pardoned by the authorities in Massachusetts.

As Stacy Schiff has explained, the excesses of the Salem trials teach us lessons that are of enduring relevance which are dusted off "whenever we overreach ideologically or prosecute overhastily, when prejudice rears its head or decency slips down the drain, when absolutism threatens to envelop us . . . Salem endures not only as a metaphor but as a vaccine and a taunt. It glares at us when fear paralyses reason, when we overreact or overcorrect."

Abraham Lincoln

[1809–65]

Unlike legends attached to many famous people, there is reliable evidence to support the story that the 16th President of the United States, was born on 12 February 1809, in a dirt floored, one room log cabin built by his father near Hodgenville, Kentucky.

His beloved mother died when Lincoln was only ten and his formal education was intermittent as he worked with his father on the family farm, before accepting labouring jobs from other farmers. Lincoln's father was brutal in his treatment of his children and left his nine year old son at home with his 11 year old sister, while he went off in search of a new wife, for what turned out to be an absence of six months. It is hardly surprising that after leaving home, Lincoln had almost nothing to do with his father.

Being largely uneducated, but skilled with his hands, Lincoln pursued numerous occupations, including work as a riverboat man, before taking up the position of postmaster in the town of New Salem, whilst also employed as a surveyor.

He developed into a somewhat ungainly and awkward man who was 6 feet 4 inches tall and appeared rather gauche and funereal in demeanour, with arms which seemed much too long for his body, "poor, lean and lank" as he described himself. He was particularly uncomfortable around women, yet he was a good storyteller and developed a mesmerising effect on audiences, despite his rather high pitched voice.

On his second attempt, he was elected to the state legislature. He expanded his voracious reading to include a study of law, leading to his admission to legal practice on 1 March 1837, after which he set up practice in Springfield, Illinois. After losing his first great love, Ann Rutledge, to typhoid fever, he married Mary Todd. He applied himself to his increasingly successful legal practice while making political speeches to raise his national profile, speaking out powerfully in condemnation of what he described as the "monstrous injustice of slavery".

Addressing a Springfield meeting in 1838, he said: "Towering genius disdains a beaten path . . . It thirsts and burns for distinction; and if possible it will have it." Not many of the 1,500 citizens of the town could have foreseen that only 22 years later their local lawyer would be elected President of the Union.

He served for three years as a US Congressman but did not make any enduring impression on Washington, before returning to his legal practice. He was unsuccessful in his attempts to be elected to the Senate in 1855 and 1859, but his fame was spreading and he launched his candidacy for higher office while delivering an address on 27 February 1860, saying: "Let us have faith that right makes might, and in that faith, let us to the end, dare to do our duty as we understand it."

Despite his limited political experience, he had aligned himself with the new industrialists who were keen to secure high tariffs to protect their markets, and he was unanimously elected as the Republican candidate for the Presidency. When the Electoral College votes ultimately fell in his favour it was portentous that he failed to receive a single vote from the ten southern states. Within weeks, the southern states had voted to secede from the Union and even before Lincoln was formally sworn in as President on 4 March 1861, at 51 years of age, Jefferson Davis had been inaugurated as President of the Confederate States of the South the previous month.

Although it has been widely accepted that slavery was the primary issue that prompted the Civil War, most historians now accept that the main driving force behind the decision of the southern states to secede was similar to the issue that had led to the War for Independence from the British: namely, tariffs, which were largely payable by the southern states who had only limited industrial capacity. It was the contribution of those tariffs which significantly increased in the years leading up to the Civil War, and which comprised the primary source of income for the northern economy, which the Southerners deeply resented. They understandably decided that when they received so little of the money they paid, they would be better off outside the Union, so that they could govern themselves.

Thus, the seeds of the disastrous conflict that ensued were more a matter of finances, because the industrialised northern economies needed the huge payments of tariffs by the southern states to fund the continuing expansion upon which their prosperity depended.

Within four months of being sworn in as President Lincoln arranged for 75,000 militiamen to be recruited and ordered that the writ of *Habeus Corpus* be suspended, enabling the military authorities to arrest and imprison without trial anyone suspected of being a Confederate sympathiser.

When a Lieutenant John Merryman was arrested without charge, Chief Justice Roger B. Taney, who had administered the oath of office to Lincoln at his inauguration, issued a writ of Habeus Corpus ordering the prisoner's release. However the arresting officer invoked Lincoln's orders and refused to comply, causing Taney to condemn the President's actions as unlawful, alleging that in usurping the power of Congress and in employing the army to carry out his purposes, Lincoln was on the road to becoming a military dictator.

After the Chief Justice had a copy of his order delivered to Lincoln, despite his training as a lawyer, Lincoln completely ignored the ruling and actually gave an order for the arrest of the Chief Justice to a US marshall for expedition. He continued to exercise his executive powers, often without consulting Congress, in order to achieve what he considered necessary to preserve the Union.

Without any approval from Congress, Lincoln authorised a huge expansion of the armed forces and established a naval blockade of the southern states, making all out war inevitable. Individual liberties were infringed and violated to an unprecedented extent and military law became paramount. By the passing of the National Currency Act, the Federal government was empowered to print and spend whatever money it required and essentially nationalised the banking system.

Lincoln issued further orders suspending Habeus Corpus throughout the country on 24 September 1862 and again on 15 September 1863, leading to infringements of civil liberties that were greater than at any other time in American history. In the first year of the Civil War alone, at least 864 people were imprisoned without charges or trial and as the war dragged on, the numbers increased dramatically, resulting in the eventual imprisonment of up to 20,000 people without trial.

> *"The human mind is impelled to action, or held in rest by some power, over which the mind itself has no control."* — Lincoln

After his death, in the case of *Ex Parte Milligan (1866),* the US Supreme Court ruled that the detention of Milligan, a civilian, under Lincoln's laws was beyond the jurisdiction of the Military Commission, and ordered his immediate discharge. The Court upheld the fundamental point that contrary to what occurred during Lincoln's Presidency, military courts and martial law only applied to areas "of military operations, where war really prevails" and had no operation over civilians when civil courts continued to operate, as they did throughout the war.

In May 1864, Lincoln ordered the army to take control of newspapers and arrested their editors and proprietors. Although some papers were allowed to resume publication after a few days, the War Department continued to impose high levels of censorship on all newspapers throughout the bloody conflict. Only survivors and deserters disclosed the full extent of the military disasters that were inflicted on the Union forces for many years. By the end of the war, he had commandeered or closed 300 newspapers in the North, because of their editorials opposing the war. Soldiers were dispatched to destroy printing presses.

The army was also sent to arrest and imprison the members of the Maryland legislature, in order to prevent them debating a Bill of Secession from the Union. Although Lincoln did convene Congress to endorse his actions, there is little doubt that many Congressmen were sufficiently intimidated by the absolute power he then wielded and did not dare to vote against him for fear of joining the ranks of those arrested and imprisoned without trial.

In prosecuting the war over the four years that followed, Lincoln assumed to himself extensive powers without the prior approval or knowledge of any branch of government, in many instances making important announcements without even consulting his cabinet colleagues. As Lincoln himself frankly admitted: "These measures, whether strictly legal or not, were ventured upon, under what appeared to be popular demand and a public necessity, trusting then as now, that Congress would readily ratify them."

Although he was correct in anticipating that most of his extra-constitutional actions would be ratified by bills passed in Congress, Lincoln could not have been confident that such approvals would be given when he took the law into his own hands. He had made some attempts to avoid war and like most of his countrymen, he was confident of a speedy resolution, but he soon realised that it was going to be a long struggle, particularly after the string of early defeats inflicted on Union forces. He then resolved to use all the resources at his disposal and employ any means necessary to achieve victory. Despite periods where he and his administration were extremely unpopular and subjected to strident criticisms, he did not deviate from his objectives or his methods.

His personal life was not without tragedy. His wife was prone to tantrums and periods of deep depression, matching her husband's. Having lost their son Edward to tuberculosis when he was only three, both parents became particularly attached to their son Willie, with whom Lincoln had established a special bond because he perceived the young boy as having "a mind most like his own".

Tragically, Willie contracted typhoid fever when only 11 years old and died in the White House on 20 February 1862. Even after the body had been removed to the morgue, the President frequently requested that he be allowed access to the coffin so that he could hold his precious son in his arms and openly wept for him. Every Thursday he closeted himself away in his son's bedroom and on other occasions Lincoln absented himself from meetings to lock himself in a room, so that he could weep alone.

Of course no description of Lincoln's life would be complete without dealing with the issue of slavery, which played an important role in Lincoln's justification of the continuing conflict between North and South. Although he had married into his wife's slave owning family,

Lincoln did speak against the institution of slavery, whilst at the same time stating that the Constitution did not permit it to be abolished. His opinions fluctuated about what should be done to address the problem. In his early years in politics, he had favoured the idea that slaves should be repatriated back to Africa to settle in Liberia, but he later realised that such a proposal was hopelessly unworkable.

He carried the document around with him for many months before disclosing its contents in his famous proclamation of September 1863, in which he stated that all persons held as slaves would be "thenceforward and forever free". As he expressed the matter in his State of the Union address later that year: "In giving freedom to the slave, we assure freedom to the free—honourable alike in what we give, and what we preserve."

Despite the understandable importance that has been attached to this proclamation, it was not issued until the war had been under way for three years and there are two critical facts that should not be forgotten about it:

Lincoln hoped to spark a slave revolt in the South by his proclamation, which, importantly, was only expressed to emancipate the slaves in the areas of the southern states over which the North had no control.

There were no slaves actually freed as a result of the Proclamation, because it did not purport to operate anywhere in the northern or border states, where slavery was also widespread. Slaves were actually used by the North to help construct the new capital in Washington.

Slavery had been outlawed throughout the British Commonwealth in 1840 and it is likely that even without the Civil War it would gradually have been phased out in America, as public opinion turned against it. Nevertheless, there is more than a touch of irony in the fact that when, towards the end of the war, General William Sherman led his Union army deep into the South after the brutal siege of Vicksburg and the utter destruction of Atlanta, thousands upon thousands of Southern civilians were sent north, along with captured soldiers, to work essentially as slaves in aid of the Union war effort. When mines were discovered on captured roads, General Sherman used Confederate prisoners to act as minesweepers. Sherman himself would certainly qualify for inclusion in our list, if we could assemble sufficient evidence of any good deeds that he performed in waging all-out war.

In his recent biography of Lincoln, Professor Thomas DiLorenzo puts forward a compelling case that, contrary to the popular perception, Lincoln was a cunning and calculating politician who subverted the Constitution, trampled on state rights and committed the North to a devastating war with the South in breach of the Constitution. He asserts that the 600,000 soldiers killed in the conflict did not die for the honourable cause of ending slavery, but rather for the dubious agenda of sacrificing the independence of the free trade southern states, in order to entrench the supremacy of a more powerful federal government, based in Washington.

Despite periods where his popularity plummeted with the repeated failures of the Union Army, Lincoln was re-elected as President for a second term in November 1864. It is now well documented that job offers and even cash payments were made to some of his opponents, to enable Lincoln to take advantage of his re-election and have passed the 13th Amendment to the US Constitution, abolishing slavery throughout the United States.

When challenged by Albert G. Hodges as to why he had reneged on his earlier promise not to interfere with slavery, Lincoln wrote: "I claim not to have controlled events, but confess plainly that events have controlled me."

No chief executive can be held responsible for every atrocity committed during all-out war, but it is worth recording that only 200 miles north of his home town of Springfield, Illinois, the notorious prisoner of war camp known as "Eighty Acres of Hell" had the highest mortality rates of any Union camp. Camp Douglas, outside Chicago, housed thousands of Confederate prisoners in overcrowded and unsanitary conditions leading to reported deaths of at least 4,454 although it only operated for a little over two years. Other estimates put the death toll at over 20%, totalling more than 6,000.

There is no evidence Lincoln was aware of the atrocious conditions, the inadequate sewerage, water supply and heating in sub-zero temperatures. But one of the main causes of death was scurvy, when Lincoln's brother-in-law Ninian Edwards had the contract to supply rations to the camp through sub-contractors.

There is also no doubt that as President he signed the order for the largest mass execution ever carried out in the United States following the Dakota Uprising in 1862. Several hundred Dakota warriors had surrendered to the overwhelming forces of the Army to end the uprising, causing them to be promptly tried in a military court and sentenced to death. Although Lincoln reduced the number to be executed to 38, it was on his orders that the warriors were hanged in December 1862, even though history supports their grievances. They were forced off their tribal lands and not paid the money promised under the treaties they had signed.

Throughout his career, Lincoln did not hesitate to use political trickery, manipulation, underhand deals and dubious promises to achieve his goals and compromised on many issues that were not indispensable to his core beliefs. At the same time he was able to project the image of an honest and dependable person, who always acted in accordance with what he considered to be the best interests of the Union. Despite the thousands of deaths and widespread suffering that he caused, Karl Marx was possibly correct in remarking that Lincoln was "one of the few men who became great while remaining good".

Although he was never a committed member of any church, Lincoln read the Bible assiduously and firmly believed in a doctrine of necessity: "The human mind is impelled to action, or held in rest by some power, over which the mind itself has no control." Such beliefs were a considerable comfort to him during the protracted conflict of the Civil War, as the casualties inflicted by Americans on their countrymen continued to mount.

He remarked to Daniel Voorhees: "Doesn't it strike you as queer that I, who couldn't cut the head off a chicken, and who was sick at the sight of blood, should be cast into the middle of a great war, with blood flowing all about me."

Ironically, his belief in a doctrine of necessity, closely resembled that of the man who assassinated him at Ford's Theatre on Good Friday, 14 April 1865, during a performance of "Our American Cousin". John Wilkes Booth was a popular actor whose fanatical commitment to the cause of the Confederacy, made Lincoln his most hated enemy. After fatally shooting the President in the back of the head, Booth recorded in his diary before his own death: "God simply made me the instrument of his punishment."

Although "Honest Abe" was one of the least experienced politicians ever to occupy the White House, his moral certitude and strongly held beliefs enabled him to guide his country successfully through the most difficult period in its history. Despite his blunders and undoubted abuse of the considerable powers he assumed, he is rightly regarded as one of the great presidents.

Lincoln had not hesitated to suspend civil rights and wage total war against his fellow Americans, in order to prevent the southern states from having the government of their choice when they seceded from the Union. Although slavery was an important issue in the conflict, it was only after the war had been waged through three bloody years that Lincoln issued his famous proclamation against it.

By the end of the conflict, more than 600,000 Americans had died on the battlefields, with more than a million wounded, and even larger civilian casualties, in a country with a population of 31 million, of whom nearly four million were slaves. The total US economy had been halved.

Perhaps the most fitting epitaph for the man and the causes in which he believed comes from memorable words he uttered amongst the graves of the fallen at Gettysburg:

> that we here highly resolve that these dead shall not have died in vain—that this nation, under God, shall have a new birth of freedom—and that government of the people, by the people, for the people, shall not perish from the earth.

Ranavalona, Queen of Madagascar

[?–1861]

The first question most readers will ask is who on Earth is Ranavalona? A perfectly reasonable question, but history tells us she was a critically important leader in the troubled history of the fourth largest island in the world, 450 kilometres east of Africa. As Queen of Madagascar, Ranavalona was undoubtedly bad, but she had some enduring, positive qualities to justify her inclusion.

The history of Madagascar is fascinating. Even though it is generally accepted that our earliest ancestors dispersed across the globe from the Rift Valley in South East Africa, there is no evidence of a human presence on Madagascar before the birth of Christ. Even more amazing is that the first humans to set foot on the island did not come from nearby Africa, but were of mixed Malay and Polynesian origin, and had travelled more than 6,000 kilometres by sea to discover the unoccupied island paradise that offered everything needed for a comfortable existence.

After unsuccessful intrusions by Portuguese, English and French colonisers, the island became a pirate haven, before it ultimately came under the control of Andrianampoinimerinandriantsimitoviaminandriampanjaka—the 23 syllable ruler who conquered the highland area of the island. He adopted Ranavalona, the beautiful daughter of a loyal subject, and arranged for her to become one of the 12 "senior wives" of the future king, his son Radama, who succeeded to the throne when only 17. As a result of a treaty he secured with the British, Radama's followers were armed with cash and the best of British muskets, in return for which he made some attempts at curtailing the slave trade, and allowed Christian missionaries into the villages, against the vehement opposition of traditionalists.

By 1828 there were almost half a million Christian Malagasy. Radama, with his superior firepower, was ruler of the island by 1825, having captured the only surviving French outpost at Fort Dauphin. At the height of his powers, his fondness for women and alcohol resulted in his death at age 36 from cirrhosis of the liver and syphilis, leaving a huge vacuum for control of the country, because he had no male heirs.

Having given birth to no royal descendants, Ranavalona realised that if she did not act quickly on the death of her husband, she would be

eliminated by Prince Rakatobe, the son of Radama's eldest sister. Before news of the King's untimely death had even been circulated, Ranavalona seized power with the aid of senior officers in the army, and on 1 August 1828, she was proclaimed Queen of Madagascar.

Rakatobe was speared to death and when his father, a provincial governor, was summoned to the capital, he was charged with deserting his post and met a similar fate, along with any other members of the royal family who could make claims to the throne, apart from the former King's only surviving daughter Salima. Even Ranavalona's lover Andrianmihaja, who had been instrumental in her ascent to the throne, was executed under her orders.

As part of the mourning tributes to the late King, the Queen banned dancing, bathing, clapping of hands, playing a musical instrument and even looking in a mirror, with perpetual slavery the punishment for anyone who breached the taboos.

At her splendid inauguration the following year, the new queen made her future intentions clear: "I will rule here, to the good fortune of my people and the glory of my name. I will worship no gods but those of my ancestors." She soon repudiated her husband's treaties and restored the slave trade that had previously made many of the locals extremely wealthy.

She assumed absolute power and introduced barbaric rites of torture, crucifixion and beheadings which had not previously been widely practised on the island. Rebels, suspected traitors and runaway slaves were flayed alive, sawn in half, or impaled on stakes erected in cauldrons filled only to waist height with boiling water so that the upper torso would remain alive and fully conscious as long as possible before death.

Suspects were tried by an ordeal known as *tanguena*. Conviction rates of 100% were achieved by gradual amputations, starting with the fingers, then the hands, feet and the limbs. As each body part was amputated, the victim would be invited to confess his guilt and only then would he be instantly executed, otherwise further mutilations would ensue.

The new regime had to deal with a determined but shortlived attempt by the French to reassert their power on the island, but following the overthrow of King Charles X, his successor, King Louis-Phillipe had no interest in Madagascar and the French forces retreated in July 1831.

Having banished all foreign forces from the island and brutally suppressed any hint of revolt amongst the locals, Ranavalona set about restoring the ancient traditions and religious practices honouring the ancestors, which had become sadly neglected. In doing so she restored a national pride in local communities and achieved some popularity despite her obvious delight in watching the cruel treatment of many of her subjects. By contrast however, when one of her favourite fighting bulls was gored to death, she was irreconcilable in her grief, and had him buried with full state honours.

She hosted lavish banquets, where thousands were fed and initiated a ceremony in which she took a royal bath (behind modesty screens) and then sprinkled her bath water over the multitudes surrounding her palace, so that her holy water would elevate her to the status of a full goddess.

Her situation was made more secure by the fortuitous arrival of Jean

Laborde, a robust young Frenchman shipwrecked on Madagascar's west coast. Upon hearing of his skills as a blacksmith who could forge cannon and muskets, the Queen wasted no time in having him appointed as her "white slave" (and lover), and showered him with gifts in appreciation of his work. With her enthusiastic support, he constructed a massive industrial complex at Mantasoa, complete with huge aqueducts and row upon row of furnaces, producing everything an advanced Western economy could supply, including muskets, cannon and grenades.

Laborde also built an incredibly ornate wooden palace for the Queen, the largest wooden structure in the world, dominating the skyline above her capital Antananarivo. Later, he constructed a huge palace that came to be known as the "Black Versailles", where the Queen and her court could pass the dry season in comfort.

After the British Government passed its *Emancipation Act* in August 1834, Britain effectively declared war on the slave trade, imposing embargos on slave trading countries including Madagascar—which still profited immensely from trading as slaves anyone who had been captured by the Queen's army. Christian communities on the island welcomed the British reform, but in doing so brought about their own destruction. The Queen's hostility to foreigners was given a substantial boost by the issue of slaves and she began to take severe measures against the Christians. who were now accused of sedition for trying to corrupt the locals into abandoning their traditional faith. They were publicly denounced at a grand *kabary,* where almost the whole population was assembled on the plains to the west of the capital. All who confessed to having converted to the new religion were required to pay a substantial fine. It had long been a custom on the island for subjects to kiss the sovereign's feet, but Ranavalona introduced a cruel variation when Christians were summoned to pay their respects—she painted her feet with poison to fatally infect the hapless victims.

Despite the hardening of her attitude against the Christians, the Queen remained obsessed with European culture and dress. The latest fashions from Paris were promptly copied and paraded at court. To the amazement of many, she appointed Laborde to tutor her only child, Prince Rakoto, who appeared to have distinctive European features. Rakoto became increasingly enamoured with European dress and habits, under the guidance of the Frenchman who was widely believed to be his father.

Before leaving the island, the last of the missionaries published a Malagasy-English dictionary and a translation of the Bible in the native tongue. But Christians could only practise their faith in secret and after the failure of a diplomatic mission sent by the Queen to the courts of England and France, persecution of Christians became more violent, more and more of the native converts to the foreign religion being cruelly executed.

Military expeditions against the Sakalava clans in the North suffered heavy defeats, but with the queen's superior firepower, the Sakalava clans knew they could not hold out against her forever. They ceded their territory to the French in return for French protection. But the French only returned to coastal islands, leaving their allies on the main island exposed to Ranavalona's rampaging army.

A rare joint operation of French and British forces to save the European traders at Tamatave resulted in a resounding defeat for the invaders. They were unable to take the heavily fortified town and returned to their ships, leaving behind 21 of their dead. Their decapitated heads were displayed on poles along the shoreline for eight years, as a warning to any *vazaha* (white-skinned foreigners) who dared challenge the Queen's authority.

"one of the proudest and cruellest women on the face of the earth . . . her whole history is a record of bloodshed and deeds of horror" — Ida Pfeiffer

---

Bizarre plans for the defence of the island were drawn up including a high wall around the whole 5,000 kilometres of coastline and an enormous pair of scissors which would somehow cut the enemy in two when they penetrated the island's defences.

In 1849, the Queen arranged the arrest and trial of over 2,000 men, women and children, including members of the royal family, for persisting in Christian worship. All were found guilty and heavily fined or sentenced to life in chains, with a final group of 18 sentenced to death. They were executed by being flung from the cliff at Ampamarinana, and their families were sold into slavery—except four nobles amongst the accused who were burnt to death. One was heavily pregnant. She gave birth to her baby as the flames consumed her and her husband. Only the Queen's favourite, Ranivo, was spared, although like the others, she had refused to renounce her new faith.

The cheerful demeanour of the Christian martyrs as they were put to death, singing their hymns together, did little to assist the Queen's campaign against Christianity, and the tide of conversions, particularly amongst the nobility, continued.

After the foreign traders paid a "fine" of $15,000 for the invasion of

Tamatave, the Queen did agree to allow foreign traders to operate on the island and the severed skulls were finally removed from the waterfront.

In 1857, when she was nearly 60, the legendary Austrian traveller Ida Pfeiffer visited Madagascar on her third tour of the world. She left the following description:

> She is certainly one of the proudest and cruellest women on the face of the earth, and her whole history is a record of bloodshed and deeds of horror. At a moderate computation, it is reckoned that from twenty to thirty thousand people perish annually in Madagascar, some through continual executions and poisonings, others through grievous labour purposely inflicted, and from warfare.

It was most unfortunate for the intrepid solo traveller to find herself caught up in an attempted coup, instigated by Frenchman, Joseph Lambert, and Laborde who had become disillusioned with the erratic queen and joined in the move to install the Prince Rakoto as the new ruler. The coup had to be abandoned in farcical circumstances, because the conspirators could not gain access to the palace.

The Queen took her time in wreaking revenge on the conspirators. It was not till two weeks later that they were charged with plotting against the Queen along with local Christians. As a result of intervention by the Queen's son, their lives were spared and their punishment was limited to banishment from the island. However the devious and vengeful Queen had devised a more subtle way to punish the conspirators, which avoided the reprisals from foreign powers that would have followed their execution. The armed escort provided for their journey to the coast enforced as many days' delay as possible in the most fever infected areas, with some of their stops lasting more than two weeks. A journey which should have taken a week was extended to 53 days. Although they all survived, by the time they reached the coast they could barely walk.

Ida Pfeiffer managed to return to her native Vienna, but she never recovered from her ordeal and died on 27 October 1858. But if the foreigners were able to escape with their lives, a very different fate awaited the Queen's subjects, with anyone suspected of Christian sympathies being subjected to the dreaded *tanguena* ordeal. Every town and village was searched and hundreds were executed. Her revenge was only curbed by her son, who tore up a list of suspected Christians which had been presented to the court to curry favour with the Queen.

On 15 August 1861, Ranavalona died peacefully in her sleep after ruling her kingdom for 33 years. Although she had been responsible for the death of at least a third of the population, she had maintained her island's independence from all foreign powers and had established a prosperous country which was not dependent on any form of foreign assistance.

In a largely peaceful transfer of power, the young Prince Rakoto assumed the throne, and wasted no time in overturning most of his mother's cruel practices, restoring land to the rightful owners and releasing captives from other areas of the island. He introduced freedom of religion and missionaries were soon re-opening schools and building new churches all over Madagascar. But Rakoto himself was deposed and allegedly assassinated. After further conflicts between rivals for throne, the French conquered the island and it became a French colony in 1896.

Ranavalona's legacy did not survive long after her death, but despite all of her cruelty and failings, the Queen had lived up to the concluding words of her address to the nation as a young queen:

> The Ocean shall be the boundary of my realm and I will not cede the thickness of one hair of my kingdom.

Aung San Suu Kyi

[1945–]

Aung San Suu Kyi has enjoyed a reputation as one of the world's most venerated and celebrated champions of democracy and human rights. Yet, despite her resounding victory in the 2015 elections in Burma, her country's Rohingya Muslims remain what the United Nations have described as the most persecuted minority in the world.

Suu Kyi's father was a general in the Burmese army who, despite his youth, became the leader of the independence movement after World War II. In 1947, when Suu Kyi was only two years old, he was assassinated by political rivals, just before the terms of Burma's independence from the British rule could be finalised. After independence, Suu Kyi's mother was appointed Burma's ambassador to India. Suu Kyi spent many years out of Burma, studying in Oxford and working with the United Nations in New York.

She lived for nearly 23 years in the UK, where she married and gave birth to two sons who have become citizens of the UK and USA. However, she decided to return to Burma to care for her mother who had suffered a stroke. Although she had remained largely apolitical, Suu Kyi was persuaded to address a pro-democracy rally in Rangoon on 26 August 1988, following which some 8,000 unarmed protesters were slaughtered in the streets by the army and security forces, which had controlled the country since a coup in 1962.

Largely because of the status of her father as the revered champion of democracy, Suu Kyi was rapidly propelled into a leadership role in the struggle to overturn the army's ruthless control of Burma. She was placed under house arrest for 15 years until her release in November 2010. During a serious attempt to assassinate her in 2003, a convoy in which she was travelling was ambushed by armed men and a number of those travelling with her were killed.

As she wrote in an essay published in 1991: "It is not power that corrupts but fear. Fear of losing power corrupts those who wield it and fear of the scourge of power corrupts those who are subject to it."

Despite all the threats against her, she continued to display a serene courage in speaking out whenever she was able, to uphold the values and freedoms she had absorbed during her time in the UK. Her increasing international profile, as the glamorously beautiful champion of

democratic rights in Burma, resulted in a number of international prizes, including the Sakharov Prize awarded by the European Parliament, the Congressional Gold Medal and the Nobel Prize for Peace.

Two days after her 67th birthday on 21 June 2012, she was afforded the rare privilege of addressing a joint sitting of the UK Parliament, where she was welcomed by the Speaker John Bercow as "the conscience of a country and the heroine of humanity".

On the same visit, she addressed a meeting at her *alma mater* in Oxford, where she described her happy years at the university: "I learned respect for the best in human civilisation . . . It gave me a confidence in humankind and in the innate wisdom of human beings. This helped me to cope with what were not quite the best of humankind."

Only two weeks before her address to the UK Parliament, ten Rohingyas were murdered in Burma's Arakan state (now called "Rakhine") in retaliation for the rape and murder of a Buddhist woman. Attacks on Rohingyas became more extensive and violent as tens of thousands were displaced from their homes. Muslims retaliated by attacking Buddhist temples and homes, before the Arakan Buddhists decided to take the law into their own hands by destroying Muslim mosques, shops and homes, forcing some 140,000 into temporary camps. Muslim residents of the city of Sittwe were forced from their homes as more than 10,000 homes were burnt down.

In the central Burmese city of Meiktila the violence was particularly extreme, often spurred on by saffron robed monks who rightly or wrongly feared that the future of their religion was under threat. In April 2013, extensive areas were burnt to the ground and when some semblance of order was restored, the rampaging mobs simply headed south, demolishing mosques and homes in more remote towns and villages. What veteran Burmese activist, Dr Maung Zarni, calls "ethno-religious nationalism" was unleashed with the full support of the military, which endorses a militant brand of Buddhism directed against the number one enemy—Islam.

After the first elections held in 2010, the military basically ignored the result, refusing to relinquish control of the country. In August 2011, Suu Kyi met with the President Thein Sein and thanks to international sanctions and Suu Kyi's standing in the West, some reforms were introduced. Hundreds of political prisoners were released and a Human Rights Commission was appointed. Censorship of the press was lifted and peaceful demonstrations were legalised. Despite these developments, Suu Kyi's fellow prisoner, U Win Tin was undoubtedly correct when he remarked: "We shouldn't be fooled by this. The military are firmly in control."

US Secretary of State Hillary Clinton, wife of the former US President, visited Burma, where she held a lengthy meeting with Suu Kyi, and in April 2012, Suu Kyi stood for election in the Kawhmu constituency in the Irrawaddy delta, winning an astounding 99% of the vote. However, she and her National League for Democracy Party (NDL) candidates were only permitted to take their seats in Parliament after swearing to uphold the Constitution they opposed, including article 59(f) stipulating that no one with children who are citizens of foreign countries can be President. The President and the speakers of both houses were former generals and a quarter of the seats are reserved for serving members of the armed forces (who attend in uniform).

When the NLD's Information Officer, Htin Lin Oo spoke out against the atrocities being committed in the name of Buddhism in October 2014, he was sentenced to two years' jail and expelled from the NLD party.

War continued to be waged against insurgents and guerrillas in the northern states of Shan and Kachin, while repeated atrocities went on against the Rohingya Muslims, whose claims for independence and basic rights as citizens continued to be denied. It is interesting that George Orwell started his working life as a policeman in colonial Burma and it is likely that he drew on the experience in his epic novel *Nineteen Eighty Four*, when he wrote that the object of perpetual war "is to keep the structure of society intact".

In his book *The Rohingyas*, Azeem Ibrahim has exposed the extent of the human tragedy in graphic terms: "A powerless minority is the victim of effective ethnic cleansing, in an environment where they are hated by their neighbours and actively discriminated against by the state authorities." They are not recognised as citizens and any identity papers previously issued to them have been confiscated, so that they are unable to leave their primitive camps.

A ceasefire of sorts was signed in October 2015, but many of the combatants simply refused to sign. When the military agreed to a further round of elections in 2015, Suu Kyi and her NLD achieved a resounding victory, securing nearly 80% of elected seats in the Lower House and over 80% in the Upper House.

Despite her success in the polls, there has been no sign of any relief for the beleaguered Rohingyas. In October 2016, Rohingya extremists attacked rural police stations in Rakhine killing nine officers. An even more lethal attack occurred on 25 August 2017, when more than 30 police stations were attacked by Rohingya radicals in northern Rakhine, killing 12 members of the security forces. As might be expected, such attacks were followed by violent reprisals carried out by the security forces.

Following the attacks of August 2017, a new campaign of violence was unleashed on the Rohingya communities in which thousands were killed as more villages were destroyed, forcing as many as 800,000 refugees to flee into the Cox's Bazaar Refugee Camp in neighbouring Bangladesh. It is estimated that more than a million Muslims have been affected by the latest crisis.

In an article published on 6 November 2017, Azeem Ibrahim wrote:

> Now, the reality of an exodus of more than 609,000 people, amounting to approximately 50 per cent of the total Rohingya population in Myanmar, in the space of one month, the incontrovertible evidence of large scale burning of villages by the Myanmar military, the reports of widespread extra-judicial killings against fleeing civilians by the country's federal security services, have made it much more difficult to avoid the conclusion that this is nothing short of genocide.

Even the young French President, Emmanuel Macron, has described the situation as "this genocide which is unfolding, this ethnic cleansing". The only criticism of the situation that Suu Kyi has been reported as expressing is: "I am not sure the government is doing enough about it." Hardly a stinging rebuke from someone whose reputation was built on championing democracy and basic human rights.

The government did commission Kofi Annan, former United Nations Secretary-General, to report on what was happening in Rakhine state, but little has been done to implement his very modest recommendations.

In trying to explain the escalating violence that has bedevilled her country, we must firstly try to understand Suu Kyi herself, who has been consistently described as somewhat egotistical and blunt with no interest in social niceties. Perhaps partly because of the long years she was forced to spend in isolation, she remains aloof and remote even when meeting foreign dignitaries.

Despite the harshness of the treatment that she and her supporters received at the hands of the military, her unbounded admiration for her father's memory has resulted in enduring ties to the army and its generals. "I was brought up to be fond of the military," she said, "to believe that everybody in uniform was in some way or other my father's son. This is not something you can just get rid of."

In fairness to her it must be recognised that even with her electoral success and international reputation, she still has no effective control over the military and is largely powerless to rein in the warring factions. The constitution she was compelled to accept specifically empowers the military to deal with all military matters. Despite her age and the wording of article 59(f) of the Constitution, she still harbours an abiding ambition to be president of her country. If she is to achieve that, she simply cannot afford to alienate those who continue to control it.

Politically she also faces a considerable dilemma, best described by Professor Ingrid Jordt: "Standing up for human rights means siding with the Muslims and not supporting the place of Buddhism in the nation. Siding with the Buddhists undermines her credibility as a human rights superstar. She has chosen to remain silent—and drawn criticism from every corner."

In a televised BBC interview conducted by Fergal Keane in April 2017, Suu Kyi said: "I am not quite like Margaret Thatcher, but on the other hand I am not Mother Teresa either."

Azeem Ibrahim asks "Is she a Nobel Peace Prize laureate or just another craven politician who will abide by 'ethnic cleansing' to not rock the boat, and allow her to stay in power unchallenged?"

Until his resignation on 21 March 2018, the President of Burma, Htin Kyaw, was a close friend and political ally, whom Suu Kyi has known since school days. It cannot reasonably be suggested that she does not "call the shots" in the civilian administration of her country, yet she continues to do nothing about the situation.

The cause of the Rohingyas has not been assisted by their adherence to Wahhabism, one of the most radical forms of Islam. Deprived of their human rights and thwarted in their attempt to obtain an independent homeland, the Rohingyas actively attempted to purge non-Muslims from areas where most of the Muslims lived.

"I learned respect for the best in human civilisation . . . It gave me a confidence in humankind and in the innate wisdom of human beings. This helped me to cope with what were not quite the best of humankind." — Aung San Suu Kyi

---

It is not surprising that their actions have been met by such brutal retaliation by the majority in the country but the fact is that neither Suu Kyi, nor anyone within the government of Burma, has been prepared to speak up for them nor take any effective steps to protect them. Whether the violence would have been avoided or even modified if she had spoken publicly against it remains unclear, but there is no doubt that she should have tried to use her popularity and standing to condemn it, just as her colleague Htin Lin Oo attempted to do in the year prior to her last election win.

In an earlier article written on 25 September 2017, the journalist Ramzay Baroud wrote: "Yet the great 'humanitarian' lost all integrity as her government, military and police began conducting a widespread ethnic cleansing operation that targeted the Rohingya, subjecting them to a brutal and systematic genocide, conducted through the Burmese military, police and majority Buddhist nationalists."

It is probably unfair to say that she is personally responsible, but she and her NLD party have a convincing majority in both houses of parliament—there was nothing to stop parliament from calling on the military to stop the genocide and if necessary, asking for international assistance from the United Nations to try to bring the violence under control. The reality is that with the Rohingyas deprived of their basic rights and wholly disenfranchised, there are no votes to be gained by such actions.

Suu Kyi has opted for sitting on her hands at the expense of her international reputation, rather than face a backlash from her own power base and deprive herself of any chance of being elected president of her country.

As our last character in Part One, Aung San Suu Kyi remains a striking example of what we have examined, providing compelling evidence that even today, there are good leaders who are prepared to allow extreme forms of evil to be perpetrated against their own citizens, when it assists them in clinging to power.

Conclusion

READERS MAY CONCLUDE THAT MY EXAMPLES are only of historical interest, of limited relevance today. But I am firmly of the view that ethical and moral issues are of enduring and universal significance. To illustrate that point we need only cast our minds back to events that followed the calamitous destruction of the World Trade Centre towers in New York in 2001.

The recently elected President George W. Bush placed America on a war footing, and terrorist suspects aligned with Al Qaeda and affiliated terrorist organisations were rounded up and interrogated using what were euphemistically described as "Enhanced Interrogation Techniques" (including water-boarding). When the practice was later made public, it was roundly condemned by his successor President Obama, Secretary of State Madeleine Albright and Democratic members of Congress as well as some CIA officers including Leon Panetta and David Petraeus.

So we chalk up one victory for the moral high ground—despite the extent of the abuses perpetrated by individual officers within the CIA, America stood for values that do not condone such reprehensible behaviour. But there are two observations that need to be made:

1. Firstly, most of the senior officers involved in the treatment that was meted out to prisoners remain firmly unrepentant about the actions they ordered or condoned. Men like George Tenet, Porter Goss, Michael Morrell, Jose Rodriguez and Michael Hayden adhere to the view that the threat to American lives that they were required to deal with justified the methods they employed, and despite findings to the contrary by a Senate inquiry, they insist that a significant body of intelligence only became available as a result of the treatment the prisoners received.

2. Secondly, in judging their actions we need to bear in mind what has happened since Barack Obama became President in January 2009. The CIA bowed to public pressure and generally abandoned attempts to capture and interrogate any of the suspected terrorists. Instead they increasingly resorted to airstrikes mainly by unmanned drones into Yemen, Somalia, Pakistan and elsewhere to summarily execute those who, according to CIA sources, were plotting against the USA.

Between November 2002 and January 2017, there were at least 643 air attacks using missiles fired from drones that can be verified according to details published on the website: www.dronestre.am. The strikes were devastatingly effective in killing thousands of people (many of them innocent bystanders) and every single attack was personally approved by the President. All but 56 of them occurred after Obama took office!

In the first reported drone attack on 3 November 2002, six people were killed in Yemen, including the Al Qaeda leader Qa'id Salim al Harithi and a naturalised US citizen, Abu Ahmad al Hijazi. On 17 December 2009, a cruise missile intended for an Al Qaeda training camp hit the village of al Majala, killing over 50 people, including 12 women and more than 20 children. Another infamous attack demolished the building in which a wedding reception was being held.

The situation came to a head in 2011 when the CIA obtained an order from President Obama to take out Anwar al-Awlaki, an American citizen who had lived in the United States for 21 years before taking up his radical stance against all things associated with his country of birth. He and three others, including another American citizen Samir Khan, were killed in Yemen as a result of a drone attack on 30 September 2011. The President's order was the first occasion since the 1860s Civil War on which an American citizen had been singled out by his own government for execution without trial. In November 2012 it emerged that in an attempt to avoid the charge of executing its own citizen, the authorities had unsuccessfully applied to strip Awlaki of his citizenship six months before his death.

During the eight years of the Obama Presidency, there were 587 attacks, averaging more than six per month. Since coming to power in January 2017, President Trump has continued the practice adopted by his predecessor and there have been 161 strikes in Yemen and Somalia alone during Trump's first 12 months in office.

So the USA has come to a position in which the capture and interrogation of suspects has been largely abandoned as unacceptable, and in its place instituted a campaign of lethal drone strikes, without any charges being laid or proven against the suspects and in the absence of any court order or even supervision of the Presidential decree.

What has happened to the high moral stance? Can the over-zealous mistreatment of prisoners really be regarded as more reprehensible than the summary execution of suspects in foreign countries, whose deaths are frequently accompanied by "collateral damage" involving the loss of other people's lives—when many if not most of the other victims were innocent of any crime, real or even suspected.

In view of the tactics that have been adopted, what complaint could America legitimately make if, in retaliation, a missile or bomb were to be detonated in the White House, the Pentagon or the CIA headquarters? There are portable missile-launchers and commercially available drones that could easily be adapted to carry an explosive device after being launched close to the target.

The other question that must be asked, is how would the CIA, the FBI or the incumbent President react if reliable information was received that a nuclear device was being assembled for detonation in a city like New York? In one of his last broadcasts before he was killed, Mahlawi confidently stated: "If you continue to send us bombs we will send bombs to you."

The technology and opportunity exist for such a device to be imported, assembled and exploded and there are numerous underpaid nuclear experts in Russia and Pakistan who would be more than willing to assist in such an enterprise. What if a terrorist involved in the project was intercepted and despite his lack of co-operation it was reliably reported that he was aware of the bomb's whereabouts? Can it seriously be suggested that the authorities would in such circumstances be morally prevented from using any of the Enhanced Interrogation Techniques, when their use could reveal the bomb's whereabouts saving millions of lives and preventing a nuclear holocaust on the US mainland?

The point I am making is that the dilemmas I have outlined from history remain as alive and relevant today as they have ever been; the only difference now is that the consequences of our actions or inactivity may be far more devastating. We need to be aware of these issues, they should be openly debated and in deciding how best to deal with them, we should heed the lessons of history.

We should remember what Aldous Huxley said: "That men do not learn very much from the lessons of history, is the most important of all lessons history has to teach us."

With those rather depressing thoughts, we now turn to the far more inspiring part of my book where we examine the tragic lives of artists whose creative urges were able to overcome huge obstacles thrown in their path, to leave us with some of the most enduring examples of the indomitable nature of the human spirit.

Part Two

Suffering Genius

Introduction

IN THE ARTISTIC FIELD, we are mercifully spared the ruthlessness and brutality we have encountered throughout history amongst military and political leaders. In fact, artists are to be complimented because they are one of the few groups over the centuries who have held themselves aloof from most major conflicts (although Hitler regarded himself as a talented artist and Churchill probably was). The artists we will come to know in Part Two are rarely involved in acts of cruelty or evil.

By the term "artist" I refer not only to painters, but also writers and composers. The common thread that links all the characters examined here, is that they endured far greater suffering than they ever inflicted. In his book *The Heart of Man*, Erich Fromm draws a helpful contrast by quoting Albert Schweitzer:

> Good is all that serves life; evil is all that serves death. Good is reverence for life, all that enhances life, growth unfolding. Evil is all that stifles life, narrows it down, cuts it to pieces.

The characters in Part One all took advantage of others and, in many cases, deprived them of life. Our second collection, despite their faults, not only showed "reverence for life", but added something worthwhile to our existence and certainly enhanced our enjoyment of it.

In his book on the conflict between Leonardo da Vinci and Michelangelo, Jonathan Jones refers to the curse of history: "For everything that is built, every beauty that is nurtured, there is a destructive warrior waiting in the wings."

I call it the "sandcastle phenomenon"—there will always be people who strive to create something original and even beautiful out of whatever material is available to them; sometimes it's the tide that comes in, but frequently it is other people who destroy it, often kicking sand into the face of the creator.

Relatively few examples of memorable art have come to us from artists living in domestic bliss surrounded by all the comforts life can provide. As Ernst Kretschmer wrote: "Peace of mind and restful emotions however, have never been spurs to great deeds." There were of course successful artists who benefitted and thrived under generous patrons, enjoying a popular and comfortable existence. But the characters whose stories appear in this book demonstrate great art being spawned out of adversity and suffering, with some degree of pain and tribulation seeming to be the most fertile area in which their art flourished.

For those whose lives we will examine, it is almost as if there is no profundity without pain. They were capable of plumbing the full depths of their artistic inspiration by being cut open and exposed to the harsh realities of the world, and it was in those conditions and in that ground that the seed of their inspiration produced the most fecund fruit. Perhaps we can use an analogy from the kitchen—with herbs like basil, the way to maximise the flavour from the leaf is by tearing it, enabling it to impart the most powerful effect into your culinary creation. The poet John Keats wrote: "Do you not see how necessary a World of Pains and Troubles is to school an intelligence and make it a soul? A Place where the heart must feel and suffer in a thousand diverse ways."

The point is illustrated by the life of Lord Byron, of whom it was said by his close friend the poet Thomas Moore: "His very defects were among the elements of his greatness and it was out of the struggle between the good and evil principles of his nature, that his mighty genius drew its strength."

Byron described poets such as himself: "We of the craft are all crazy. Some are affected by gaiety, others by melancholy, but all are more or less touched."

The experience of Virginia Woolf provides a further illustration of how fruitful a life of distress and even madness can be in producing creative writing. "Madness can afford the individual certain resources and abilities that are not available to others," writes Jeffrey A. Kottler in his recent book *Divine Madness—Ten Stories of Creative Struggle*. "The fantasy life, free flight of ideas, distortions of reality, and heightened senses . . . offer a unique perspective on the world."

Kottler lists ten poets, 14 other writers, and many composers, actors and musicians of the 20th century who suffered debilitating depression or bipolar disorder. He points out that while the incidence of manic-depressive illness is about 1% in the general population, amongst artists and writers, it is as high as 38%. Amongst adults whose lives demonstrate a level of creative genius, well over 60% experienced fully fledged mental illness. It is not that all artists are mad, but there is a close relationship between some mental illnesses and the creative process.

As Kottler explains, most artists have to live with some form of pain and suffering and in order to survive, they become adept at channelling and converting their troubles in a way that enables them to be fruitful in their areas of creativity. If they are able to cope, they often excel by finding an explanation and an expression for their pain.

As Edgar Allan Poe admitted: "Men have called me mad, but the question is not yet settled whether madness is, or is not, the loftiest intelligence—whether much that is glorious—whether all that is profound—does not spring from disease of thought, from moods of mind exalted at the expense of general intellect."

If Poe is right, the price we may already have paid for the tens of thousands of children (mainly boys) who have been administered mind-altering drugs like Ritalin for treatment of ADHD and similar disorders, may be that we have stifled some of our most creative minds in attempting to curb their behaviour.

Before examining examples of troubled artists, it is helpful to try to understand where artistic originality comes from. The answer is as varied as the artists themselves, but some generalisations can be made. In his excellent book *The Genesis of Artistic Creativity*, Michael Fitzgerald writes:

> Creative artists must have extraordinary levels of energy and motivation, and a tremendous capacity for observation and concentration . . . They must have a vast curiosity and be driven to understand the world in an artistic way, and also to rebel and go against the orthodox artistic mode of expression of their time.

They are frequently discontented and conflicted, compelled to rely on their imagination to build bridges between their inner and external world. Fitzgerald quotes Steptoe, who described the artistic personality as "hypersensitive, aggressive, autonomous and independent, pre-occupied with work to the exclusion of social activity, intolerant of order and seeking novelty and change, suffused with intense but chaotic emotions, and opposed to the conventional and the banal".

Exploring the link between genius and madness, he suggests that many artists work as intensely and imaginatively as they do in order to remain sane. Access to aspects of the mind's functioning that is unavailable in more staid and conservative lives gives their work its flair and sense of risk. More than 350 years ago John Dryden wrote:

> Great Wits are sure to Madness near allied
> And thin Partitions do their Bounds divide.

No amount of training or practise can replicate what makes an individual genius so originally creative, but it is beyond the scope of this book to establish the factors that give rise to such originality. Some artists had symptoms of autism and/or Asperger's syndrome. Some, like Beethoven, endured handicaps in the very area of creativity they worked in. Others were manic depressives. Many had physical ailments and illnesses.

Like their violent or cruel counterparts in Part One, our artists were able to apply *Whatever It Takes* to create their original contributions. It is their success in overcoming whatever afflicted them which qualifies them for inclusion in this book.

Aristotle was probably the first to draw the connection between depression and creativity after noticing that most poets were melancholic. His observations from more than 2,300 years ago are reinforced by the artists we will examine. I make no claim to being a psychologist or psychiatrist and proffer no diagnoses in what I outline. There are symptoms associated with conditions like manic-depressive illness and bipolar disorders which are referred to, but I do not pretend to explain why these people behaved in the way they did. My aim is to try to ascertain what befell them and outline what they were able to achieve or create despite their afflictions, without attempting any psychoanalysis of them.

There are many individuals whose case studies demonstrate that their creativity was enhanced by their mania, leading to what Kay Redfield Jamison wrote: "Creative people see farther and wider; their cognitive peripheral vision is clearer; they make connections between seemingly disparate things that many of us miss."

Although there are exceptions amongst my characters, I also agree with the statement by the psychiatrist Nassir Ghaemi who wrote: "When not manic or depressive, those with bipolar disorder are normal, just like everyone else, but they retain an awareness that makes their perception just different enough to be unusually creative."

Whatever the diagnosis may be in each individual case, we should not underestimate the extent to which these conditions debilitate the sufferers, requiring them to endure an excruciatingly painful and miserable existence, devoid of hope, with death often seen as the only way out. That they were able to find an outlet for their suffering in what they created, is one of the marvels of human nature.

In his thoughtful article on why the "tortured artist" is not a myth, Christopher Zara wrote: "Art is a reflection of humanity, and humanity's greatest virtue is its ability to overcome adversity." Zara's approach to art is part of what inspired this book and it dovetails neatly with the historical philosophy of Arnold Toynbee, who in his 12 volume *A Study of History*, published after the Second World War, explained that: "Man achieves civilisation, not as a result of superior biological endowment or geographical environment, but as a response to a challenge in a situation of special difficulty, which rouses him to make a hitherto unprecedented effort."

I have found no evidence in the lives of artists in this book that their mental condition was ever worsened by their creative work. In fact the madness seems to feed the inspiration and provide the artist with a reason to live. Although some psychiatrists oppose the suggestion, artists like van Gogh and Virginia Woolf certainly believed that it was their pain and suffering from mental disorders which inspired their creativity. In many other instances, the creative work seems at least to hold the condition at bay whilst the work is undertaken. There is frequently a relapse when the inspiration is exhausted.

In her meticulously researched book *Touched with Fire*, Kay Jamison outlines a "compelling association" between the artistic and the manic depressive temperaments, emphasising the importance of moods in igniting thought-changing perceptions and enabling apparent chaos to be transformed into something original. She points out that in many instances, artistic work which is inspired by or executed in a manic state may be successfully edited or refined when its creator is less depressed or has reverted to something closer to normal.

As she explains the phenomenon, there is a tension between opposing emotional and cognitive states in artists, which plays an important part in their creative processes. She even cites examples where artists have been able to use their art to heal themselves. Although mental disorders such as manic depression have enormous destructive potential for all of us, especially for the more sensitive, they can be the source of heightened imagination, intensified emotional responses and increased artistic energy.

The struggles of the individuals concerned, and what they were able to create despite the tragedy of their lives, provides us all with inspiration for what can be accomplished under even the most challenging circumstances. Our artists, amongst many others we have not dealt with, are all proof of the capacity of even a deeply troubled human being to apply *Whatever It Takes* to overcome handicaps and create art that has in every case enhanced our lives.

One of the most inspiring aspects of humanity is that someone like Franz Schubert could produce some of the most sublime chamber music and songs ever written, while suffering from extreme poverty, social isolation and the worst symptoms of venereal disease. He had only a limited circle of friends who were interested in his music, and his only public concert occurred less than a year before his death aged 31 years.

Schubert recorded a remarkably perceptive insight into his own condition, and the broader theme of this book, in his diary in March 1824: "Pain sharpens the understanding and strengthens the mind; whereas joy seldom troubles itself about the former and softens the latter or makes it frivolous."

Similarly Vincent van Gogh—who sold only one painting and worked for years without recognition or reward to produce masterpieces that are treasured amongst the world's most valuable paintings—had to contend with every form of adversity, including mental illness: "I am risking my life in my work," he said, "and half my reason is gone."

Yet he remained true to his unique artistic inspiration and continued to paint right up until his death at age 37.

Amongst our artists we will find some like Milton, Toulouse-Lautrec, Byron and Beethoven, who were cruelly handicapped by physical afflictions. Beethoven, Schumann, van Gogh, Virginia Woolf and Hemingway battled with debilitating mental disorders. Many like Gauguin and Baudelaire forfeited comfortable lives in pursuit of their artistic inspirations. Baudelaire and our final artist, the twentieth century writer Charles Bukowski, relied on their squalid living conditions to inspire their writing.

All our artists suffered from depression, some to a severe extent and many were suicidal at times in their lives. Van Gogh, Gauguin, Woolf and Hemingway took their own lives. Tchaikovsky also battled with depression and profound feelings of guilt and confusion because of his homosexual urges. Physical ailments, including advanced syphilis, ruined the lives of Schubert, van Gogh and Baudelaire. Yet all were able to lift themselves clear of their handicaps and troubles to leave their inspirational legacy for our enjoyment. Not only should we be grateful for the sacrifices they made, but their triumphs should inspire us.

Although I am deeply indebted to all of the authors whose books I have used, I am particularly appreciative of the work done by two of the writers I have relied upon in compiling Part Two:

Jeffrey A. Kottler for *Divine Madness—Ten Stories of Creative Struggle* and Kay Redfield Jamison for her inspirational book *Touched with Fire*.

As our first example of creativity in adversity, we start with some of the earliest art that has come down from deep in the past when, as far as we know, writing and music barely existed.

The Altamira Cave Paintings

[15,000–35,000 YEARS AGO]

When *Homo sapiens* was still struggling to overcome the threat posed by the stronger and larger species of Neanderthals, people were surviving in primitive cave dwellings, where with fire they could cook food and keep wild animals at bay. Danger and hardship were a daily part of their lives, yet in one of those caves, located in Northern Spain, close to the village of Santillana del Mar, are some of the most amazing paintings from the Palaeolithic era more than 15,000 years ago.

Extending 296 metres into the depths of the cave, the Altamira site is best known for its superb painted ceiling, but its galleries and chambers contain an abundance of engravings and paintings in which we can still see vivid depictions of wild animals, human hands and abstract signs and symbols, the meaning of which has long disappeared. Although in the modern era prehistoric paintings have been found at Chauvet and Lascaux, the Altamira paintings were discovered first and are some of the oldest and most beautiful images created by our Stone Age ancestors.

The Great Hall is a high-vaulted space which includes some compartmentalised quadrilateral signs in red along with black and red figures. On the ceiling there are striking depictions of 18 bison, a horse and an impressive hind, 2.5m in length. The natural contours of the rock are cleverly employed to depict some animals curled on the ground.

Applying charcoal, manganese and ochre to the walls, together with red and even violet pigments, the artists depicted over a hundred animal images in extraordinary detail, meticulously representing even the texture of fur on their skin and the flowing manes of movement. They even managed to create a three dimensional effect in the drawings, brilliantly utilising the natural contours of the cave walls. Natural rock shapes were transformed into humanoid faces by the addition of eyes and other details to create a series of remarkable "masks". The artists somehow managed to apply a range of what we would describe as artistic techniques, with advanced drawing skills, shading, painting and even engraving some images to achieve dimensionality, naturalism, abstraction and symbolism.

As Simon Busch accurately described them, the paintings are "The Sistine Chapel of Palaeolithic art".

Because the art is vulnerable to moisture and pollution, the cave is

closed to the public. After it became a UNESCO World heritage site in 1985, a detailed replica of the cave was installed in a new museum on the site. The museum has faithfully and sympathetically reproduced the polychrome paintings, showing us detailed depictions of bison, horses, deer and striking hybrid creations of humans with animal heads.

The name most closely associated with the Altamira paintings is Marcelino Sanz de Sautuola who was shown the site by a local hunter in 1868. It was in fact his young daughter Maria who first chanced upon the extraordinary paintings when she attended the cave with her father in 1879. When news of the exciting discovery was released, the artistic skill displayed in the works was so impressive that experts of the day declared they were modern forgeries. It was not until many years later, after Marcelino had died that the world was prepared to accept that such artistic masterworks had in fact been created by Palaeolithic people.

They are now generally recognised as dating from as early as 35,000 years ago, through to about 15,000 years ago when the most recent additions were made. Somehow the paintings have retained brilliant colours, and there is none of the childish images or immature effects that we generally associate with early attempts at art. It is as if the painters emerged without prior experiment as fully fledged and highly accomplished artists.

In his book *Cave Art*, Bruno David makes the telling observation that the earliest of the paintings date from the beginnings of the Ice Age when primitive man was locked away in the caves for months at a time to survive while conditions were too harsh outside. Living and working in pitch black conditions, it would also have been necessary for the family groups, including the artists, to defend the cave from the bears whose bones are still visible within the complex, as well as the larger and stronger Neanderthals who still roamed in the area.

"after Altamira, all is decadence" — Pablo Picasso

As David wrote, Altamira, "though a silent reminder of a distant people or a relic of a long-gone past, continues to speak to us today and to draw our imagination about how we fit in a much grander world."

Since the discoveries of Altamira, cave art has been identified in every continent except Antarctica. Similar images have been discovered in the spectacular caves of Chauvet and Lascaux in France, where brilliant depictions of bison, deer, horses and cattle appear to race across the rough stone surfaces in wild profusion. Some are in black outline, but many others are completed with vivid colours, showing a striking resemblance to real life, in a style surprisingly similar to the paintings at Altamira.

By a technique used also in the much cruder images created by the indigenous artists of Argentina and Northern Australia, the Altamira artists blew coloured pigments onto their hands flattened against the wall, to create silhouetted shapes, usually blowing through hollowed out animal bones. In South Africa's Blombos caves, archaeologists have discovered a prehistoric artist's workshop where mixtures of pigments and ochres dating from an even earlier period can still be found on the cave floor.

If we take a moment to contemplate the physical circumstances of those cave dwellers, battling for survival in a hostile and dangerous environment, their achievement in creating wonderful images deep within the darkest recesses of the cave, is nothing short of miraculous.

Pablo Picasso summed it up perfectly after he visited the cave at the height of his international success: “None of us could paint like that; after Altamira, all is decadence.”

Michelangelo

[1475–1564]

From the Ice Age in northern Spain, we leap into the turmoil and creative intensity of Renaissance Italy. One of the artistic giants of the era was Michelangelo di Lodovico Buonarroti Simoni, born on 6 March 1475 in Caprese near Arezzo in Tuscany. As a young man he displayed exceptional talent as a painter and sculptor. His father was infuriated by Michelangelo's obsession with drawing and frequently tried to deter him by corporal punishment from pursuing a career as an artist. Lorenzo the Magnificent recognised Michelangelo's precocious talents as a sculptor and allowed the young man access to his private garden and the opportunity to copy some of the prized classical pieces in his collection.

Michelangelo's favoured treatment and prodigious talent aroused resentment amongst fellow students at the Humanist Academy in Florence, and at age 17 he was brutally punched in the face by the local bully, Pietro Torrigiano, leaving him with a broken and badly deformed nose. He never recovered physically from the incident and was haunted by it psychologically for the rest of his life.

During the next 62 years until his death in 1564, he excelled as a sculptor, painter, engineer, architect and poet, leaving a phenomenal quantity of inspirational work which cemented his reputation as one of the most original and gifted artistic geniuses of history. He not only sculpted the San Lorenzo tombs and statues and painted the ceiling of the Sistine Chapel, but also designed the new Campidoglio in Rome and the Biblioteca Laurenziana or Laurentian Library.

His most moving sculpture is probably the "Pieta" depicting the Virgin Mary holding her dead son Jesus collapsed across her lap, which is now displayed behind heavy security glass in St. Peter's Basilica, the only sculpture that bears his signature. When the statue was unveiled to an astonished world in 1499, the art historian Giorgio Vasari said "It is certainly a miracle that a formless block of stone could ever have been reduced to a perfection that nature was scarcely able to create in the flesh."

Criticised for depicting the Virgin Mary as too young and beautiful to be Christ's mother, Michelangelo countered by pointing out that it was sin that caused people to age and therefore the Immaculate Virgin would not show her age like other people.

But his most famous sculpture is the 18 foot tall statue of David with his slingshot draped effortlessly over his left shoulder which stood for centuries in front of the Palazzo Vecchio in Piazza della Signoria in Florence, before being replaced by a copy. The original moved into the Gallery of the Academia. The enormous block of marble that Michelangelo used had been rejected as fatally ruined when Simone da Fiesole drilled a hole through the legs of the figure at the wrong height. The block was transformed by the genius of Michelangelo, creating a relaxed yet confident figure with one knee cocked, so that his weight is transferred to the other foot. The result is widely regarded as the most perfect depiction of a male nude, combining a pose of serenity and grace, imbued with latent strength, arguably surpassing every other sculpture ever created, both ancient and modern, or at least equalling the best.

Although he was 23 years younger than the other great Renaissance man, Leonardo da Vinci, it is extraordinary that two of their most famous works were first sighted less than 12 months apart in Florence when Michelangelo's David was unveiled for the first time on 8 September 1504 not far from da Vinci's most famous painting "La Giaconda", better known as "the Mona Lisa".

"For everything that is built, every beauty that is nurtured, there is a destructive warrior waiting in the wings." —Jonathan Jones

---

The records show that a vicious and irreconcilable enmity prevailed between the two men. Leonardo described his rival's sculpture as "a most mechanical exercise often accompanied by great sweat, compounded with dust turning to mud". When the leaders of Florence met to decide what to do with Michelangelo's statue of David, Leonardo produced a cruel caricature of the sculpture, showing a belligerent thug with a beaky profile. He took it upon himself to address the meeting and suggested that the statue would best be located in a corner of the covered loggia, where it would not interfere with the "ceremonies of the officials". With words even more devastating for the young sculptor, in a vicious assault on the power of the statue's virility, Leonardo also insisted that it required an *ornamente decente* to cover David's genitalia, even though Leonardo had freely painted nude figures throughout his career.

Although the statue was eventually erected in the public space of the Piazza della Signoria, Leonardo's other suggestion was followed and its power was diminished for some time by the brass thong draped around its waist to which were attached 28 copper leaves to preserve its modesty.

As previously noted, in his book on the conflict between Leonardo da Vinci and Michelangelo, Jonathan Jones refers to the curse of history: "For everything that is built, every beauty that is nurtured, there is a destructive warrior waiting in the wings."

The conflict between the two great geniuses came to a head when Leonardo's contract to paint a mural on the wall of the Great Council Hall, depicting the Battle of Anghiari, was overshadowed by a commission granted to Michelangelo to install a painting at the other end of the same wall, celebrating another great Florentine victory, at the Battle of Cascina.

The competition between the two men became a spectacle that drew artists from all over Italy and elsewhere, to admire the heights of originality and artistic genius that they attained in their rivalry.

Neither painting has come down to us, and they were probably never completed, but we can still see the sketches and cartoons both artists prepared before starting work. Although their rivalry must have created considerable tension in the workspace, they may not have worked at the same time, because Leonardo applied for and was granted a period away from his work, in order to accept a commission to work in Milan, and Michelangelo was summoned to Rome by Pope Julius II to commence work on statues for his monumental tomb.

The Florence Gallery contains a number of powerful but unfinished sculptures that were originally amongst the 40 commissioned by the Pope for his tomb in Rome. In their rough-hewn state, you can see the figures transformed by Michelangelo's genius, as they appear to be struggling to escape from each crude marble block.

When his beloved Florence was threatened Michelangelo gave his energies to reinforcing the city's defences and designing and constructing war machines to repel the attackers. His efforts enabled Florence to withstand a ten month siege in 1529–30, before it was eventually compelled to surrender to the Papal and French forces.

When the Republic was overthrown and the Medici family restored to power in Florence in 1530, Michelangelo was on the list of those who were to be executed. After hiding out in the city, his life was spared by the intervention of Pope Clement VII before the assassins could find him.

In his landmark publication, *Lives of the Artists*, Michelangelo's former apprentice, Giorgio Vasari, does not attempt to disguise the fact that he regarded Michelangelo as the greatest artist and most admirable man of his time. He wrote that the Almighty was dissatisfied with the "worthlessness" of 15th century art, so he sent into the world "an artist skilled in each and every craft", including painting, sculpture and architecture. Moreover he was endowed with "the knowledge of true moral philosophy and the gift of poetic expression, so that everyone may admire and follow him as their perfect example in life, work and behaviour, and in every endeavour, and he would be proclaimed as divine".

If we bear in mind that Vasari was writing of a period when Leonardo da Vinci was in his prime, along with other outstanding artists, such as

Piero Della Francesca, Mantegna, Giotto, Donatello, Ghiberti and Andrea Del Verrocchio, his is high praise indeed.

As Vasari mentioned, Michelangelo was also a talented poet, who wrote over 300 sonnets and madrigals and was also an outstanding architect and engineer who designed the Medici Chapel and the Laurentian Library as well as redesigning the Piazza Campidoglio at the top of the Capitoline Hill in Rome, which became the first planned square of modern times. His talents also led to him being entrusted with the design of the fortification of the hill of San Miniato, which dominated the city of Florence.

Michelangelo's paintings and murals are far too numerous to mention individually. His most outstanding achievement as an artist was the 500 square metres of ceiling he painted over four exhausting years in the Sistine Chapel, which has continued to stun the world since it first opened on 31 October 1512. In his book, Vasari dedicated ten pages to describing the wonders of the ceiling. Michelangelo was not unique in attempting to synthesise the Platonic traditions of ancient Greece within the framework of Christian beliefs, but what made the ceiling so exceptional was the sheer scale and beauty of his achievement in its iconographic layout. It is astonishing still, in the way the great artist managed to graft voluptuous paganism to Christian asceticism.

It was Pope Julius II, a great admirer of Michelangelo's work, who prevailed on Michelangelo to undertake the ceiling of the Sistine Chapel as well as to create a magnificent tomb for himself, decorated with sculptures. Julius died before the project could be finished.

Although he made no secret of the fact that he much preferred to be working at sculpture rather than painting, Michelangelo worked on his own in the chapel for more than four years to create what many regard as the greatest single work of art in extremely arduous conditions. Painting above his head on uncomfortable scaffolding must have severely taxed his stamina and strength.

When Michelangelo asked the aggressive and warlike Julius, how he would like to be portrayed, the Pope is said to have replied: "Put a sword in my hand for I would not know how to hold a book."

The tomb had different problems. Negotiations for its completion dragged on for decades, as the scale of the project shrank further and further after the Pope's death, causing Michelangelo to lament, "I have wasted all my youth chained to this tomb."

Michelangelo's physical appearance seemed indomitable, and his contemporaries applied the word *terribilita* ("frightening power") to his work. But his life was rendered at least uncomfortable and on one view, absolutely miserable, by those who plotted against him. His work and reputation were constantly denigrated, not only by Leonardo, but by other prominent and influential men, like the architect Bramante and the artist Raphael, who were jealous of the range of talents that Michelangelo brought to his work.

Despite his prolonged period of fame, he always lived frugally, being utterly devoted to his art and religion. His pre-occupation with the male nude has led to speculation that he was homosexual, and it is true that in his 50s he wrote love sonnets to a handsome young nobleman, Tommasi Cavalieri. There is no reliable evidence to contradict his denial of ever engaging in sexual activity with men, and we may accept that the love he declared was a celibate one. He was always extremely pious and never wavered in the practice of his faith, being described by his contemporaries as *Il Divino* ("The Divine One").

He never married and his longest sustained relationship was with the poet Vittoria Colonna, to whom he addressed many of the hundred or more sonnets that place him at the peak of romantic poetry of his day. Sculpture was his greatest passion however and there is some truth in the observation that his pictures are sculptures in paint.

Michelangelo returned to the Sistine Chapel in 1536 and spent a further five years completing the immense fresco of the Last Judgment above the altar. When Pope Paul III insisted on inspecting the painting before it was finished, his adviser Biagio di Cesena condemned it for its depiction of male nudes in such a sacred place. Michelangelo had his revenge however, as the fresco has remained uncensored, including a depiction of Biagio in the depths of hell with other devils, trapped by an enormous serpent wrapped around his legs.

Some of Michelangelo's last great pictorial works are his frescoes in the Pauline Chapel in the Vatican. In them we can recognise the artist's tragic mood, provoked by the suffering of the world in which he lived.

After completing the Last Judgment when he was 75 years old, his last major project, which he reluctantly undertook in his 80s, was to take over Antonio da Sangallo's position as chief architect for the construction of the basilica and dome of St. Peter's. Michelangelo modified Bramante's original plans for the interior and designed the higher, lantern-topped dome which towers over the building. Although his design was further modified after his death, it remains one of his crowning achievements.

His life was a constant battle against those who wished to censor images of nudity, who regarded him as *inventor delle porcherie* ("the inventor of obscenities"). He also had to deal with the political instability of his time, and cater for the whims and changing priorities of the numerous popes and other patrons who were highly unpredictable in the support they provided. His creative life extended through the lives of five popes. Yet despite the patronage he enjoyed, he was never wealthy because he sent much of the money he earned to support his aging father and other family members, and rarely allowed himself periods of idleness or rest.

He died just before his 90th birthday in 1564, and even at the end of his long and productive life, he famously said: "Ancora imparo"—"I am still learning."

John Milton

[1608–74]

John Milton lived and wrote in one of the most revolutionary periods of English history—when a king was beheaded and religious and political conflict was an almost daily event. At Cambridge University as a young student, Milton established himself as a poet of note in Latin verse. However, after travelling to Italy, he returned to England when it was on the brink of Civil War during the reign of King Charles I.

For nearly 20 years following the outbreak of the conflict in 1642, Milton abandoned poetry in favour of political activism, becoming increasingly embroiled in the Republican movement. He fearlessly published controversial pamphlets and papers, writing passionately in favour of divorce and free speech. Long before Voltaire, in a publication which remains powerfully relevant today, Milton wrote: "Give me the liberty to know, to utter, and to argue freely according to my conscience, above all liberties." (*Areopagitica*, 1644)

Even before the King's infamous trial and execution at the hands of the Rump Parliament, Milton had published a treatise calling for the abolition of the monarchy and the execution of the King. In return, Cromwell arranged his appointment as the well-remunerated Secretary for Foreign Tongues and he thereafter worked enthusiastically as a promoter of the new regime, despite clear evidence that soon began to emerge that one form of tyranny had only been replaced by another.

His wife Mary died three days after the birth of their daughter Deborah, and worse for Milton, his only son Ralph died six weeks later. Earlier he had noticed a rapid deterioration in his eyesight and by age 44 he was totally blind. His blindness and personal tragedies were all the more incapacitating for Milton, because he accepted the prevailing view that such disasters were punishment from a God in whom he fervently believed. His condition not only rendered him unable to write without an assistant, but worse still, he was unable to continue his voracious reading in Latin, French, Greek and Hebrew, apart from what was read to him.

His second wife Katherine died giving birth as well, to his fourth daughter, who died before she was 5 months old.

With Cromwell's death in September 1658, his Protectorate began to unravel, particularly under the incompetent and inexperienced leadership of Cromwell's son Richard, who succeeded him.

On 29 May 1660, King Charles' son returned to London in triumph and set about restoring the monarchy and revenging himself against all who had plotted against his father. Most of the leaders of the Republican movement were brutally executed and many were surprised that Milton's name was not amongst the condemned. Milton was nevertheless forced into hiding and later arrested and imprisoned for some months.

Disillusioned with politics and devastated by his personal losses, he returned to poetry. Despite the very real threats he still faced because of his outspoken views, the enemies he had made over the years, and the increasingly intolerant religious and political climate that prevailed after the Restoration, Milton was able to draw on his vast knowledge of both the classics as well as less conventional scholarship, to produce one of the epic masterpieces of the English language: his ten book poem in blank verse, *Paradise Lost*. Extending over 10,000 lines, the poem describes Satan's revenge in tempting Adam and Eve in the Garden of Eden, resulting in their banishment and the creation of evil and sin.

As Anna Beer wrote in her biography of Milton: "*Paradise Lost* is a great achievement in itself but an even more remarkable one for an elderly blind man living in a world of persecution and plague."

He accepted the view that such disasters were punishment from a God in whom he fervently believed.

Within the epic poem, we find a quotation applicable to both parts of this book:

That all this good of evil shall produce,
And evil turn to good; more wonderful
Than that which by creation
First brought forth
Light out of darkness.

Economic hardship compelled him to sell his library and his difficulties were exacerbated by chronic glaucoma, extremely painful gout, and kidney failure. His domestic situation had also deteriorated as although he was able to marry a third time, his daughters had ceased to care for him. Evidence adduced at the trial following his death, when his family disputed his will in the courts, indicated that his daughters had totally abandoned him for some years, despite his disabilities.

Notwithstanding all the tragedies and problems he faced, and despite the constant threat of censorship or worse, Milton continued to write some of the most inspiring poetry of all time, dealing with eternal themes of good and evil. He managed to combine fervently religious stories with political and social commentary that is still relevant today.

Paradise Lost did achieve some success during Milton's lifetime, despite condemnation by many of those who had returned to power. They knew only too well the message Milton was so successful in communicating through his brilliant literary output, although lines in *Paradise Lost* are equally applicable to his hero Cromwell:

Who overcomes by force
Hath overcome but half his foe.

This masterpiece was followed by other poetry including *Paradise Regained* and *Samson Agonistes*, but eventually the strain of his ailing health led Milton to cease writing and, shortly before his 66th birthday, he died in his home, only a short distance from where he had been born.

Ludwig van Beethoven

[1770–1827]

Born into a musical family on 16 December 1770, Beethoven is rightly regarded as one of the giants of classical music, who changed music forever through the power and originality of his compositions. One of the best descriptions of his work is contained in his own words: "Music should strike fire from the hearts of men and bring tears from the eyes of women."

By the time he composed the first of his nine symphonies however, he had already lost 60% of his hearing and despite trying every suggested cure, his hearing inexorably declined, leaving him totally deaf for his last 11 years.

In September 1787 he wrote "I have been suffering from melancholia, which in my case is almost as great a torture as my illness." In a letter to his friend, Karl Amenda in July 1801, he wrote: "know that my noblest faculty, my hearing has greatly deteriorated . . . of course I am resolved to rise above every obstacle, but how will it be possible?" In another letter from the same period, he lamented:

> For two years I have avoided all social gatherings because it is impossible to say to people "I am deaf." If I belonged to any other profession it would be easier, but in my profession it is a frightful state . . .

For many years he lived in hope that his condition would at least be arrested if not improved, but he soon realised that there was nothing that could save his hearing, causing him to become so frustrated that he wrecked his favourite Graf piano, because he could not hear a note of his own music. Conversations could only be conducted with people using books to write out their speech to which Beethoven was then able to respond. No wonder he was described by one of his contemporaries, Ludwig Cramolini, as "Old cross-patch".

Beethoven was born in Bonn, where the grandfather after whom he was named worked as Kapellmeister of the Elector's Court. His father was a music teacher and a tenor in the Court Kapelle, but he did not approve of his young son improvising on the violin and piano before learning the discipline of playing correctly, resulting in Beethoven suffering regular beatings during his childhood.

He gave his first concert performance as a seven year old on 26 March

1778 and published his first composition at age 12. He was sent to Vienna in 1786 to further his musical education but, after the death of his mother in 1787, his abusive father sank deeper into alcoholism, leaving Ludwig to support and care for his two younger brothers.

As a performer, he had mastered the violin, organ and horn, but his greatest love was always the piano.

While Haydn and Mozart were still alive, Beethoven moved to Vienna and although his reputation was initially based upon his performances as a piano virtuoso, he soon began to play his own compositions. The structure of his early compositions faithfully followed classical traditions of the two great masters, but he was already introducing what one reviewer described as "dangerous originality" into his music, with his own distinctive flourishes of a new romanticism.

He had a difficult time with the elderly Haydn, who remarked of his young pupil, "You make upon me the impression of a man who has several heads, several hearts and several souls."

He made his debut as an orchestral composer on 22 November 1795 and by 1800 he was conducting his Symphony No 1 as well as his Piano Concerto in C, which were enthusiastically received by his Viennese audience. The Empress Marie Therese became a supporter of his music, but her husband did not share her enthusiasm. "There is something revolutionary in that music," said the Emperor, rightly concerned.

In 1800 he fell in love with his beautiful young pupil, Countess Guicciardi, but the difference in their ranks made any lasting relationship impossible. His feelings were beautifully reflected in one of his most famous pieces, the "Moonlight" Sonata in C Sharp Minor, which he dedicated to her.

He was described as "plain-looking with an ugly red, pock-marked face" with hair that "hung almost shaggily around his face". He had small "fiery eyes . . . that were deep set and unbelievably full of life". John Russell on observing him playing the piano, said "The muscles of his face swell and its veins start out; the wild eye rolls doubly wild; the mouth quivers and Beethoven looks like a wizard, overpowered by the demons he himself has called up."

In 1802, he moved from Vienna to Heiligenstadt in an attempt to improve his health, composing his last will and testament as he wrote to his brothers of his increasing despair and suicidal thoughts, which he was only able to overcome by resolving to continue living through his art. The letter included the following heart-rending passages:

> for 6 years now I have been hopelessly afflicted, made worse by senseless doctors, from year to year deceived with hopes of improvement finally compelled to face the prospect of a <u>lasting</u> malady . . . If at times I tried to forget it all oh how harshly was I flung back by the doubly sad experience of my bad hearing. Yet it was impossible for me to say to people, "Speak louder, shout, for I am deaf."
>
> How could I possibly admit an infirmity in the one sense which ought to be more perfect in me than in others, a sense which once I possessed in the highest perfection . . . My misfortune is doubly painful to me because I am bound to be misunderstood; for me there can be no relaxation with my fellow-men, no refined conversations, no mutual exchange of ideas . . . I must live alone almost like an exile.

Even in the depths of his despair as his hearing declined, he was able to produce his brilliant and energetic Second Symphony, as well his first 12 piano sonatas and his first six string quartets. It was as if his music was able to emerge from some higher plane that was somehow isolated from his physical and mental energies. His deafness not only interfered with his conversations and his enjoyment of music, but it also rendered him increasingly incapable of pursuing success as a public performer, losing part of his identity as well as reducing his income.

Although he was able to continue performing for a few more years, the only positive aspect of his tragic circumstances was that he no longer had any reliable capacity to do anything other than compose and so he threw his immense energies and genius into composition. He only overcame the depths of his despair by the strength of his determination, driven by romantic ideals and dedication to his art as a composer.

Beethoven also suffered from tinnitus, chronic intestinal disorders and diarrhoea, as well as attacks of colic. He had liver problems and after his death the autopsy disclosed that he suffered from advanced cirrhosis of the liver from his prodigious consumption of alcohol as well as renal papillary necrosis. There are less reliable reports that he also suffered from syphilis and lead poisoning from its treatment.

> *"The muscles of his face swell and its veins start out; the wild eye rolls doubly wild; the mouth quivers and Beethoven looks like a wizard, overpowered by the demons he himself has called up."* —John Russell

Despite all these obstacles, for the next 25 years his genius continued to produce epic works that are amongst the most powerful creations in the history of music. On frequent walks through the countryside, he was seen growling and howling as he threw his arms about in time to the music in his head, stopping occasionally to make a pencil note of particular passages he wanted to record, before resuming his walk.

He was originally a supporter of Napoleon and his republican views and had dedicated his third "Eroica" symphony to him. When he heard that Napoleon had betrayed all republican principles, to have himself crowned Emperor, Beethoven tore out the dedication page in a fury, ripped it in two and threw it on the floor, dedicating the work instead to his loyal patron, Prince Joseph Franz von Lobkowitzy.

By the time of the premiere of his Third Symphony in April 1805 however, he was suffering from recurring fevers, painful abscesses in his jaw and finger, month long headaches and long standing episodes of vomiting and diarrhoea, on top of his rapidly diminishing hearing. He suffered speech and language difficulties and frequently limited his conversation to monosyllabic responses. He became increasingly bad tempered and frequently offended the patrons upon whom his livelihood depended.

In a letter to one of his patrons, Prince Lichnowsky, Beethoven was presumptuous enough to point out: "Prince, what you are, you are by accident of birth; what I am I am of myself. There are and there will be thousands of princes. There is only one Beethoven."

Although he is principally remembered for his monumental nine symphonies and piano concertos, he also wrote an opera, numerous piano and chamber music pieces together with an impressive collection of religious music. His later music was as revolutionary as the French Revolution he supported.

He attempted to pass himself off as a member of the nobility, but was eventually compelled to abandon the pretence, after his deception was exposed in court. He became increasingly obsessed with death and suicide, suffering acute periods of depression and anxiety, which found reflection in many of his epic compositions. It was his music, however, which remained his most effective anti-depressant, and it was almost certainly his abiding inspiration as a composer that saved him from taking his own life.

The attention span of the Viennese public must have been far superior to our own, because on 22 December 1808, Beethoven premiered his monumental Fifth Symphony, his Sixth Symphony "The Pastoral", the Choral Fantasy, Piano Concerto in G, Op 58, and several movements of the Mass he had composed for one of his other patrons, Prince Esterhazy.

In May 1809, when the invading French army began bombarding Vienna, Beethoven was so concerned about damaging what hearing he had left, that he hid for days in the basement of his brother's house, covering his ears with pillows to try and deaden the noise of the cannons.

By 1816, he was completely deaf and thereafter he never heard a note from any of his most memorable compositions. Although for most people, deafness is not regarded as the worst affliction, for a man like Beethoven, whose whole existence was dedicated to music, it must have been the source of almost unbearable pain, as indicated by the passage quoted earlier from his Heiligenstadt letters.

As he became increasingly deaf, he also became more irascible and petulant, discarding friends and insulting even his most dedicated patrons and supporters, as well as alienating any woman who interested him. Ill humoured and anti-social even before his hearing disappeared, he failed to establish any lasting relationship with a woman at any stage of his life, partly because he was so indifferent to his own slovenly and dishevelled appearance.

Music was his sole preoccupation and he was frequently composing three or four works at the same time. Although he laboured over his work, he was amazingly adept at providing impromptu variations on any theme given to him to the delight of his listeners. But, like other composers of his time, he was constantly frustrated by finding pirated copies of his music in circulation and was frequently in conflict with his publishers.

Although his output suffered during periods of acute illness, he continued composing despite failed attempts to find happiness in his love life. Unfortunately for the great composer, most of the beautiful young women he fell for were members of aristocratic families and despite their shared enthusiasm for music, there were no realistic prospects of any of them being permitted to join Beethoven in his life as a humble composer.

He also became embroiled in a protracted legal dispute over the custody and care of his nephew Karl, prompted by his firm conviction that his sister-in-law was not a fit mother for the young boy after the boy's father died of tuberculosis. Like so much else in Beethoven's life, his success before the courts and his fondness for the boy were never appreciated and his nephew continued to treat his uncle with barely disguised contempt, accumulating enormous debts before attempting suicide and ultimately joining the army.

His last public performance occurred on 7 May 1824, when he conducted the premiere of his epic Ninth Symphony, the "Choral" Symphony at the Kartnertortheater in Vienna. Because of Beethoven's deafness, the orchestra was instructed to only follow the baton of the assistant conductor, Michael Umlauf, and at the end of the performance Beethoven had to be gently turned around to face the audience by one of the singers, so that at least he could see the tumultuous applause that greeted the performance of his greatest masterpiece. Despite its success, many in the audience found the work beyond them, and Beethoven was so disappointed in the profits from ticket sales, he accused those close to him of defrauding him.

As one of the reviews by Carl Czerny recorded at the time: "so much power, innovation and beauty as ever came from the head of this original man, although he certainly led the old wigs to shake their heads".

Increasingly bedridden, Beethoven wrote that he was "living an unhappy life in conflict with nature and the Creator". Yet he continued to compose, including completing his last string quartets. In addition to his other health problems, he developed pneumonia, jaundice and dropsy, before dying on 26 February 1827 at age 56, during a violent thunderstorm that was said to closely echo the dramatic storm effects that had been created by the composer in his Sixth Symphony ("The Pastoral").

Although it is perhaps apocryphal, his last recorded words were:

> I shall hear in heaven.

The poet Franz Grillparzer said in Beethoven's funeral oration:

> The thorns of life had wounded him deeply. He withdrew from his fellow-men after he had given them everything and received nothing in return. He remained alone because he found no second self. But until his death he preserved a human heart for all men, a father's heart for his own people, the whole world. Thus he was, thus he died, thus will he live for all time.

George Gordon Lord Byron

[1788–1824]

Speaking on behalf of all poets, George Gordon, better known by his titled name, Lord Byron, wrote: "We of the craft are all crazy. Some are affected by gaiety, others by melancholy, but all of us are more or less touched." Coming from families who on both sides had histories of suicide and extravagance, Byron was certainly "touched" and struggled from a young age with severe bouts of depression and mood swings, as well as being acutely conscious that he had been born lame.

Mary Shelley, the second wife of his close friend Percy Bysshe Shelley, wrote: "No action of Byron's life—scarce a line he has written—but was influenced by his personal defect." Kay Jamison describes Byron's life in *Touched with Fire*:

> Heir to madness, virulently melancholic, and in lifelong fear of going insane. Byron represents the fine edge of the fine madness—the often imperceptible line between poetic temperament and psychiatric illness. His terrible struggles with melancholy and his "savage moods", yet his work's indebtedness to them . . .

Although he eventually inherited a substantial estate and a title which enabled him to take his seat in the House of Lords, Byron was born with a clubfoot in a rented room off Oxford Street in London in the year and month that his countrymen claimed the continent of Australia—January 1788.

Before Byron's father, Captain "Mad Jack" Byron, met Byron's mother, he eloped with Lady Camarthen and had a daughter, Augusta, who was to feature prominently in Byron's adult life. Byron's mother, Catherine Gordon, was a Scottish heiress descended from James I of Scotland, but "Mad Jack" soon depleted her fortune and fled to the continent to escape his creditors, paying only scant attention to his sensitive and very gifted son, before dying when Byron was three.

As a young boy, Byron was sexually abused by his Scottish nurse. He was educated at Harrow School and then Trinity College, Cambridge University. As a result of many failed attempts to cure his clubfoot, he had become a strong swimmer and he also took part in boxing contests and played cricket. Although there is no record of him ever attending a lecture, he graduated with a Master of Arts degree in 1808. His first collection of poems *Fugitive Pieces and Hours of Idleness* appeared in 1807 and he was soon recognised as an extraordinarily gifted writer. But he was also extremely eccentric at Cambridge, where, when informed that university regulations prevented him keeping his favourite dog, he acquired a tame bear and delighted in parading the animal through the town on a leash, because bears were not included in the regulations.

After coming of age, he took his seat in the House of Lords in 1809, but having fathered a child with one of the maids at his ancestral home, and incurring enormous debts, he followed in his father's footsteps and departed for the continent in June 1809. He managed to avoid Napoleon's rampaging army and spent much of his time in Greece before returning to London on 14 July 1811.

After returning from his first "Grand Tour", he was overwhelmed by the death of his mother and three close friends and sank into a deep depression, although he had already completed the first two cantos of his largely autobiographical poem *Child Harolde's Pilgrimage*, soon to make him famous. In a letter to his friend Francis Hodgson on 13 October 1811, he describes his life: "My days are listless and my nights restless . . . I don't know that I shan't end with insanity."

Having inherited the title Lord Byron, he attended the House of Lords a total of 48 times and spoke on two further occasions after delivering his maiden speech on 27 February 1812. But it was the publication of his completed poem which made Byron an instant celebrity, lionised by aristocratic and literary London. His melancholy hero, an outcast from society touring foreign lands, is closely based on his own character and experiences, and has become one of the most recognisable Romantic figures of the era.

However, Byron's personal life staggered from one scandal to the next after he had a brief but tumultuous affair with Lady Caroline Lamb, the wife of future Prime Minister Lord Melbourne. She famously described Byron as "mad, bad and dangerous to know". Further affairs followed with Lady Oxford, Lady Frances Webster, and most scandalous and enduring of all, with his half-sister Augusta, who was married with several children.

Despite these scandals, he married Annabella Milbank on 2 January 1815, but predictably the marriage was a disaster for both of them and within a year they had separated. The bailiffs entered his house and sold his library, and his wife and newborn daughter Ada returned to her family. He left for the continent in April 1816, ordering an extravagant travelling coach with sleeping accommodation, despite enormous debts, departing England for the last time.

After the publication of the third canto of *Child Harolde's Pilgrimage*,

Sir Walter Scott wrote:

> There is something dreadful in reflecting that one gifted so much above his fellow-creatures, should thus labour under some strange mental malady that destroys his peace of mind and happiness, altho' it cannot quench his genius . . . Suicide or utter insanity is not unlikely to close the scene.

In lines from the same canto of *Child Harolde's Pilgrimage*, we read an apt description of the poet himself:

> The apostle of affliction, he who threw
> Enchantment over passion, and from woe
> Wrung overwhelming eloquence.

After visiting the Waterloo battlefield and spending time in Switzerland, Byron settled into a riotous life in Venice where he started writing *Don Juan* following a prodigious number of sexual encounters with what was estimated to be over 200 women, despite the fact that he had grown uncharacteristically obese with "a pale, bloated and sallow complexion". When the first two cantos of *Don Juan* were published anonymously in 1819, it was denounced as "a filthy and impious poem . . . from the Satanic school", but Byron was encouraged by the praise it received from Goethe. The great German writer also praised Byron's *Manfred* poem of 1817.

"mad, bad and dangerous to know" — Lady Caroline Lamb

In 1819 he was introduced to Teresa, the 19 year old Countess Guiccioli and despite her married status, he managed to seduce her in a gondola a few days later and they became lovers. Incredibly, Teresa's husband allowed Byron to reside with Teresa in his Palazzo in Venice, where Byron managed to shake off his depression and complete *Don Juan*, loosely based on his extraordinary life. He also completed three classical dramas for the stage and other scandalous pieces.

But his mental torments continued, particularly after he lost his young daughter Allegra in the same year his close friend Shelley drowned. He described himself as subject to "violent paroxysms of rage" waking every morning "in actual despair and despondency".

In 1821, a Committee had been formed in England to organise aid in support of the Greek battle for independence and, knowing Byron's enthusiasm for their cause, they approached him for assistance. In July 1823, he left Italy to help the Greeks fight the Turks, spending time in Cephalonia before eventually arriving in Missolonghi in January 1824. He funded the insurgents' cause and formed the "Byron Brigade" but failed to achieve any military success before April 1824, when he contracted a severe chill after being soaked to the skin, leading to rheumatic fever. He died on 19 April 1824.

In one of his last poems, written at Missolonghi on 22 January 1824 to celebrate his 36th birthday, he wrote:

My days are in the yellow leaf
The flowers and the fruits of Love are gone,
The worm in the canker, and the grief
Are mine alone.

Because of the many scandals he had been embroiled in during his colourful life, the Dean of Westminster refused to allow him to be buried in the famous Abbey. Although there were more than 40 carriages in his funeral procession, they were mostly empty, because even after his death, most of the aristocracy did not want to be associated with his name.

For much of the 19th century, Byron was lionised as the ultimate romantic hero, who epitomised the melancholic wanderer who gave his life in the cause of freedom. In reality he was a flawed hero, who led a dissipated and self-indulgent life, paying no regard to the values of his contemporaries. He was however, a literary genius, who was able to draw on his own experiences in a process of self-revelation that both astounded and shocked his readers.

Earlier in his literary career, he had written what is an appropriate epitaph for himself within canto 10 of *Don Juan*:

> In the Wind's Eye I have sailed, and sail, but for
> The stars, I own my telescope is dim;
> But at least I have shunned the common shore,
> And leaving land far out of sight, would skim
> The Ocean of Eternity

Franz Schubert

[1797–1828]

Unlike most great composers of his time who made their reputations in Vienna, Schubert was born in the Lichtenthal district of the city and lived there for most of his short life. Although his father was a keen amateur musician, he was determined that his son should follow him into the teaching profession. But no one could ignore the outstanding musical talent of the young Schubert, who could play the piano, organ, violin and viola by age 11, enabling him to be accepted into the Imperial Court Chapel. Here he received further musical education under the elderly Italian composer Antonio Salieri, who had also taught Mozart and Beethoven. Salieri did not however approve of Schubert's interest in setting German poems to music.

Under pressure from his father, he was compelled to work as an assistant teacher at his father's school, but he hated every minute of it and was frequently found absent from his position so that he could give his attention to composition. He was placed in charge of the lowest class of children who were determined to learn nothing and forget whatever they had been taught. Yet even in his miserable circumstances, Schubert was still able to produce some of his most inspiring music, penning more than 100 songs, half a dozen operas and operettas, several symphonies, church music and numerous chamber music pieces.

He ultimately abandoned the job in 1816 and thereafter dedicated himself to working full time as a composer. Despite the quality and originality of the music he produced, his compositions were virtually unknown outside his small circle of friends and Schubert never succeeded in attracting a rich patron or even a paying audience.

He was also affected by the political climate under Prince Metternich, who ruthlessly suppressed all dissent in the capital, and increased levels of censorship led to Schubert's arrest in 1820.

Schubert was short and corpulent (only 5 foot 1 inch) and was extremely shortsighted. Described as timid and almost childlike, he nevertheless had a passionate commitment to his artistic genius, despite his limited recognition. He suffered from almost continuous headaches and giddiness and, after contracting syphilis, became almost housebound as the illness became more and more insidious, leading to patchy hair loss and an unsightly red rash.

The worst of his symptoms were probably precipitated by the mercury treatment he endured, producing difficulties swallowing, drooling, diarrhoea, vomiting and excess urination. As well as the effects of heavy drinking, Schubert also suffered from cyclothymia, a mental illness producing severe mood swings and acute depression.

In a letter to his friend Leopold Kupelwieser, he wrote: "I feel myself the most unhappy, most wretched being in the world . . . for every night when I go to sleep, I hope that I may never wake again, and every morning renews the grief of yesterday."

Despite serious health issues and a desperate financial situation, Schubert produced over 1,000 cheerful and profound compositions, ranging from symphonies (eight that were completed), chamber music and his inspired songs, which numbered more than 600. He also composed operas and operettas, but none of them were ever performed and he even used some of the scores to light a fire to keep himself warm.

His life is the embodiment of the romantic artist: living alone in poverty, with appalling health, composing miraculous and uniquely melodic music that was virtually unheard during his short life, outside his modest circle of loyal friends.

In the letter of 31 March 1824, where Schubert describes himself to Kupelwieser as most unhappy and wretched, he adds, "whose most brilliant hopes have perished, to whom love and friendship have nothing to offer but pain."

"every morning renews the grief of yesterday" — *Schubert*

Although 27 years younger than Beethoven, he lived for only 20 months after Beethoven's death. They both lived and worked in Vienna, but Schubert was so overawed by his renowned hero, that he never plucked up the courage to approach him, even though they both frequented Bogner's Coffee House, where the brooding and intimidating figure of Beethoven often sat sullenly in the corner.

Schubert was granted an audience with his hero in 1822, but after Beethoven pointed out an error in the harmony of his Piano Variations, Schubert was so mortified that he could not utter a word and left in despair. Shortly before Beethoven's death on 26 March 1827, he was supplied with a selection of Schubert's songs, which apparently delighted the maestro, causing him to belatedly praise the young man: "Truly in Schubert there is a divine spark." After paying the dying man a final visit, Schubert was allowed to occupy the position of a torchbearer accompanying the coffin at his funeral.

In his last year, Schubert's friends were able to arrange the only public performance of some of his music at The Musikverein of Vienna on 26 March 1828 to commemorate Beethoven's death. Tragically, it clashed with a Paganini concert, and as a result the concert was not even reviewed.

He continued to compose, producing what are probably his finest collections of songs in *Die Schone Mullerin*, while hospitalised in the Vienna General Hospital for treatment of syphilis. His last song, "Shepherd on the Rocks" was completed only three weeks before he died. He also wrote his great String Quintet in C Major and his A Major

Piano Sonata D 959 during these final months and we only need to listen to the slow movements of both works, interwoven with a pervading and profound melancholy, to appreciate the depths of despair to which he had been reduced.

In his last letter to his friend Franz Schober he wrote: "I am ill, I have eaten nothing for eleven days and have drunk nothing. I totter feebly and shakily from my chair to bed and back again. Rinna is treating me; if ever I take anything I bring it up at once." Rinna was his devoted 13 year old sister, but despite her best efforts, Schubert died on 19 November 1828 from a combination of typhoid poisoning and tertiary syphilis, aged only 31.

With no money for a funeral, it was only after a posthumous performance of his music that enough money was raised for a memorial to be erected in his honour, lying in the same cemetery as Beethoven, inscribed with words penned by his friend Grillparzer, the same poet who had penned Beethoven's funeral oration:

> Death buried here a rich possession. But yet fairer hope.

Robert Schumann

[1810–56]

Robert Schumann achieved considerable fame and material comfort during his productive life, but he always struggled with mental disorders that produced frequent outbursts of anger and at least one suicide attempt on 27 February 1854, when he flung himself into the near freezing Rhine River in Dusseldorf, only to be rescued by local fishermen.

Schumann was born on 8 June 1810 in Zwickau, the year Napoleon's troops marched confidently through the town on their way to Moscow, before the devastated survivors of the disastrous campaign returned, defeated and diseased.

His father was a prosperous publisher but as the youngest of five children, Schumann was profoundly affected by the suicide of his sister Emilie and the death of his father when he was only 16.

From a young age he displayed exceptional musical talent, particularly his ability to improvise, but his mother did not support his musical interests and he was compelled to enrol as a law student and compose in secret. His early work comprised mainly songs and piano pieces, including a highly original quartet for piano and strings. He also began to pursue a career as a concert pianist, but an injury to his right hand ruined any chance he might have had as a performer, although it did enable him to avoid military service.

He suffered his first major anxiety attack at 18, when he was convinced he had been buried alive. He became increasingly afflicted by hypochondria, fearing cholera and tuberculosis as well as the constant threat of a looming insanity. He described himself as "Available for everything but fit for nothing" and attempted to overcome feelings of anxiety and depression with cigars and alcohol. Twice he set his bed on fire when he fell asleep in an inebriated state, still smoking his cigar.

Schumann was also a gifted writer and poet dealing largely with autobiographical themes. He invented two characters for himself, Florestan, the masculine, out-going side of his personality and Eusebius, the sensitive, artistic side. He even employed the two characters in his work as a music critic and editor of a successful newspaper, providing insightful music reviews.

In October 1833, the death of his brother and favourite sister-in-law Rosalie produced a total breakdown with panic attacks and suicidal

obsessions. But he became increasingly fond of Clara Wieck, the 14 year old daughter of his music teacher, whose outstanding ability as a concert pianist led to her performing all over Europe as well as composing original songs and piano works. Gradually they developed a relationship, despite vehement opposition from her father, who did everything in his power to keep them apart. Schumann brought a lawsuit against his future father-in-law, enabling them to marry on 12 September 1840.

Despite inner torments, his beautiful and talented wife inspired him to write some of his best music, much of which she performed at her hugely successful concerts. In 1840 alone, he composed over 128 songs as well as other pieces for piano. With his wife's encouragement he also began composing orchestral pieces, including his first symphony, and later an opera, "Genoveva". Although she had eight surviving children during their 13 years of marriage, Clara was able to continue her illustrious career as a concert pianist.

Schumann was frequently unwell, suffering from attacks of dizziness and high blood pressure. He suffered another major breakdown in 1844 and continued to be afflicted by massive mood swings and periods of depression. He found it increasingly difficult to accompany his wife on her extended concert tours, with some professional jealousy understandably present, when his work as a composer was constantly overshadowed by her popular successes.

While living in Dresden, the city was overwhelmed by a bloody revolution, but the Schumann family managed to escape and despite all his afflictions, Schumann continued to compose, apart from those periods when his symptoms completely overwhelmed him.

"Available for everything but fit for nothing" — Schumann

The family moved to Dusseldorf in September 1850 when Schumann obtained the position of musical director, despite his obvious shortcomings as a conductor, resulting in one embarrassing occasion when he continued to conduct even after the choir had finished. He completed a number of new religious works as well as his "Rhenish Symphony" (No. 3 in E Flat Major), which remains one of his most popular pieces.

As well as conflicts with his employer, Schumann was suffering from debilitating sciatic back pain and began to experience disturbances in his speech, often with auditory hallucinations. He completed his "Fantasy in C Major for Violin and Piano", as well as his "Concerto for Violin and Orchestra", but the tunes he struggled to record became increasingly drowned out by the flood of inner voices and his depressed mood became more and more overpowering. Angels singing divine music became harsh voices of demons making horrible music, with tigers and hyenas rushing to devour him.

At 43 years of age, Schumann was a distinguished composer, music critic and director, but his mood swings became more unmanageable and enduring, causing him to plunge into the almost frozen waters of the Rhine while the city was in the midst of the Fasching Carnival celebrations. After being rescued, he made a further attempt to drown himself, before he was sent to a private clinic at Endernich, near Bonn where he remained for his last three years, where his wife was permitted to visit him only once. Increasingly inarticulate, alone and refusing to eat, his health rapidly declined and he died on 29 July 1856 at the age of 46.

Despite all the physical and psychological problems that had bedevilled him, Schumann produced an enormous body of musical and literary work, which inspired many composers and writers after him. As Tchaikovsky wrote of him a few decades later:

> With the shadow of his insanity already hanging over him, this inspired poet of human suffering seemed incapable of finding those moments of tranquillity in which he could establish an objective relationship to his music.

Charles Baudelaire

[1821–67]

Baudelaire was the first major writer to build his artistic reputation on his self-destruction. Later French poets like Corbiere, Rimbaud and Mallarme, shared a common pattern of poetic inspiration derived from hardship, addiction and encroaching insanity, but Baudelaire was the first. As his biographer Alex de Jonge wrote:

> The art of that time was born of disaster, as if the artist who sought to capture its spirit could only do so by stretching his nerves beyond breaking point and building his art from the pieces of a shattered self.

Baudelaire's father had been a priest, who had been elevated to the position of sub-deacon in the Church of St. Denis in Paris, but abandoned his vocation at the time of the French Revolution. He survived the Napoleonic era and married for a second time in 1819 aged 60, to Caroline Dufay, who gave birth to their only child, Charles, on 9 April 1821. Unfortunately, his father died when Charles was only six. His mother remarried after falling for the dashing army officer Colonel Jacques Aupick, who moved the family down to Lyons, where Charles was enrolled in the local military school, which he predictably hated.

By the time he returned to School in Paris, Baudelaire was already writing poetry, but disappointed his teachers because of his "butterfly mind" and was expelled in 1839. He was already describing his *ennui*, a self-loathing, disgust and emptiness, causing a feeling of moral and functional paralysis, preventing him from attending to all that most needed his attention. So he decided to be a writer, with only his step-father foreseeing what lay ahead: "Let him be a poet and a dandy if he wishes, as long as he doesn't draw his inspiration from the gutters."

Tragically, as a result of what was probably his first sexual encounter with a "red-headed beggar girl", he contracted gonorrhoea and by 1841 he had what was then incurable syphilis, and with it an increasing dependence on a cocktail of drugs, requiring him to make repetitive and unrelenting demands for money, particularly from his successful half-brother Alphonse. As would happen so often in his life, he became increasingly estranged from his mother after she learnt of the extent of his indebtedness and his immoral and self-indulgent lifestyle.

His step-father attempted to lure Baudelaire away from his degenerate

life in Paris by paying for him to travel to the Far East, but the journey ended in Mauritius and he returned to Paris after eight months away, completely infatuated with his "Black Venus", Jeanne Duval, who became his first and most enduring love. Despite her cruel treatment of him and her repeated unfaithfulness, Jeanne inspired much of his best poetry, and even later when they were both completely impoverished, he would always somehow find money for her.

At 21, he received a substantial inheritance, which could have enabled him to live a comfortable life if managed responsibly, but Baudelaire was dedicated to the life of a stylish but profligate dandy, who always spent more than he had. He soon found himself having to change hotels repeatedly to avoid his many creditors. His increasing addiction to laudanum and hashish, as well as his extravagance, led him to explore the most depraved and degenerate vices, which he publicly flaunted to shock and scandalise his conservative contemporaries.

Despite his declining fortunes, he dedicated himself to a life of luxury and elegance, freely writing promissory notes for any item that appealed to him, without regard for cost. At the same time, he became preoccupied with the macabre, the depraved and the morbid, all of which he rejoiced in and luridly described in his poems, along with erotic themes. As he recorded in his journal: "It is through leisure that in part I developed. To my great detriment, for leisure without a fortune creates debts, and the humiliation that results from debts."

"I am killing myself because I am useless to others and dangerous to myself." — Baudelaire

He did begin to establish a reputation as a critic and became an enthusiastic champion of the paintings of Delacroix, but his name was most often associated with extravagance than with literary output for many years. He never contemplated taking any form of regular employment and relied upon his increasingly destitute state to inspire the works he continued to produce.

Baudelaire's eccentricity is demonstrated in a story of him leading a purple lobster on a leash through the Latin Quarter of Paris. He always insisted on living in the style of one of his contemporaries, Privat d'Anglement, who despite being penniless, required his battered boots to be polished by the shoe-shine boy, who politely asked Privat: "Shall I also polish the toenails?"

His decadent waste of his inheritance prompted his family to appoint a conservative and bumbling lawyer called Ancelle, as his *conseil judiciare,* to manage his money. Ancelle's cautious approach infuriated Baudelaire for the rest of his life. He always hoped that his writing would save him financially, but despite his boundless optimism, he never attained any widespread readership until after his death.

He wrote to his mother at the time: "Ancelle has administered the last rites. So that all that remains is for me to withdraw into myself and wrack my brains." In a letter from the same period he wrote: "As you know I have been seriously ill. My stomach has more or less been ruined by laudanum, but it is not the first time and I will survive."

Despite his optimism, he made a serious attempt to take his own life by stabbing himself in a restaurant in June 1845, leaving a note: "I am killing myself because I am useless to others and dangerous to myself." But his attempt did prompt a reconciliation with his family, which was short lived as Baudelaire explained to his friends that his step-father served only claret and he was a Burgundy man.

As well as his poetry, he managed to write excellent art criticism, including a spirited defence of the Romantic Movement, emphasising that its essence contained a new range of emotional experiences, with the modern, more neurotic man, reacting to the hostility of the world around him, by withdrawing into his conflicted self.

Although he continued to find inspiration for his writing, he found it increasingly difficult to marshall the energy and concentration he needed to comply with deadlines and meet the demands of the few sources of remunerative work he was able to garner. His notorious lack of punctuality was not assisted by removing the hands from his clock, replacing them with the words: "It is later than you think."

He continued to make demands on his guardian and his mother in increasingly desperate letters including one in which he wrote:

> For idleness kills, devours, consumes me. I really do not know how I have the strength to cope with the disastrous consequences of that idleness, and still retain total intellectual lucidity and a perpetual hope for wealth, happiness and peace . . . Frankly laudanum and wine are poor ways to fight unhappiness. They pass the time but do not rebuild your life. Besides it takes money to stupefy yourself.

Although by nature he sympathised with the aristocracy, he sided with the revolutionaries in 1848 and even helped to man the barricades before Emperor Napoleon III regained power, further alienating many of those who may have been inclined to support him.

The 1850s were "years of quiet despair". The cocktail of drugs and alcohol he continued to consume affected not only his productivity, but also started to affect his health, including the loss of his hair. As he wrote to his mother: "I think there can be few examples of a life as dilapidated as mine".

Baudelaire was a great admirer of Edgar Allan Poe, whose writings he began to translate into French. Yet his greatest achievement was his ability to create marvellous poetry despite the miserable and desperate plight in which he lived. He sent anonymous poems to the beautiful and imperious courtesan Apollonie Sabatier, but when he eventually admitted his infatuation, he was so shocked by her enthusiastic response that he disappeared—he could only live in the world of his imagination and couldn't cope with the raw emotions that came with a love affair in real life.

He was also besotted with the actress Marie Daubrun, who inspired a collection of poems. In one of the most famous, "*L'Invitation au Voyage*" ("Invitation to the Voyage"), he invites her to accompany him on a journey to the Spice Islands because:

La, tout n'est qu'ordre et beauté,
Luxe, calme et volupté
[There, everything is only order and beauty
Luxury, peace and sensuality]

There he imagined an escape from creditors and his miserable existence, which caused him to move frequently, sometimes six times a month. Marie rejected him and his attempt to return to his "Black Venus" was rebuffed.

A meticulously edited collection of his best poems was eventually published in 1857 under the title of *Les Fleurs du Mal* (The Flowers of Evil), but they were widely condemned, and Baudelaire was cruelly portrayed in one cartoon as the "Prince of Putrefaction". The authorities not only confiscated the book but also prosecuted the author, the printer and the publisher, for impropriety. After Baudelaire wrote an importuning letter to Empress Eugenie, his fine of 300 francs was reduced to 50.

As the title suggests, it is a book detailing the flowers of evil, in which Baudelaire goes out of his way to shock and scandalise, glorifying the grotesque and the macabre. It also contained lyrical pieces that were brutally honest and, although he drew heavily on his own experience, he went beyond the personal to describe universal themes and truths that still resonate with readers today.

Baudelaire's genius lay in his ability to transform the misery and depravity of his life into vivid writing that is graphic and uplifting. His poems are testament to the fact that he regarded poetry as a spiritualising process, where the poet is lifted out of his squalid existence by the purity of his inspiration.

When even the optimistic Baudelaire realised his poems would never gain him the recognition and wealth he craved, he was shattered and became increasingly angry with the world. At the same time he gradually began to realise that although only 36 years old, he had wasted his life and squandered the opportunities that had been provided to him.

He continued writing however, and was the first in Paris to publicly praise the music of Richard Wagner as well as minor artists such as Meryon. He also wrote a much maligned treatise on hashish and opium titled *Les Paradis Artificiels.* Although he probably intended the book as a warning against the dangers and ultimate futility of all addictions, he wrote so graphically of the effects induced by the different types of drugs that it probably helped to create the drug culture amongst many artists that followed after him.

His health began to deteriorate even more, with severe bouts of depression, stomach pain and persistent vomiting. Despite being continually hounded by his creditors he still found money to assist his "Black Venus", who was destitute and had suffered partial paralysis.

With so many creditors, he was changing hotels almost daily and eventually fled to Belgium where he delivered some singularly unsuccessful lectures. By the time he returned to Paris, he had lost his hair, and was suffering from vertigo and speech disorders. Like his beloved Jeanne, he also had paralysis of his right side and was soon unable to speak at all. His mental condition had deteriorated to such an extent that he couldn't even recognise his oldest friends.

Eventually, he died in his mother's arms on 31 August 1867, with a smile illuminating his tragic face. He was 46 years old. Baudelaire had written his most fitting epitaph as part of the Epilogue to *Les Fleurs de Mal* in which he describes the effect that Paris had on his writing:

Tu ma donne ta boue
Et j'en ai fait de l'or.
(You gave me your mud
And I made it into gold.)

Pyotr Tchaikovsky

[1840–93]

Although Tchaikovsky was born into an era of political oppression in Russia, under Tsar Nicholas I, the intelligentsia had begun to thrive with literary giants like Pushkin, Dostoevsky and Turgenev emerging at the same time as the uniquely Russian music of Glinka. Tchaikovsky's father was an engineer who had been appointed Chief Inspector of Mines in Votkinsk, but he was also an accomplished flute player. His mother Alexandra played the piano and sang, so it was not surprising that their second child Pyotr began to display his interest in music from a young age after his birth in 1840.

He was frequently found tinkering on the piano and on one occasion he was tapping out a tune on a window pane with such vigour that the glass broke, causing a serious laceration to his hand. After hearing music played during a party hosted by his parents, he was found sitting up in bed, crying. When asked what was troubling him, he replied: "Oh this music, this music! Take it away! It's in here (striking his forehead) and it won't let me sleep."

He was given music lessons, but as a young boy, his energies were given more to writing on religious topics and he allocated time every day to reading the Bible—a habit that endured for the rest of his life.

When his family moved to St Petersburg, he was placed in a boarding school, but being an abnormally sensitive and shy boy, he was constantly miserable and frequently ill. He became so distressed by his mother's departure, that he threw himself at the turning wheels of her carriage to try to prevent her leaving. He blamed himself for the death of one of his few friends, when he unwittingly infected him with scarlet fever. He was devastated by the death of his mother from cholera when he was 14 years old and probably never fully recovered from losing her.

After finishing school he enrolled in the School of Jurisprudence and graduated in 1859, taking a position in the Ministry of Justice. By this time he was aware of his homosexual preferences and it is interesting that in the graduation photograph, he is the only student with his arm interlocked with the young man next to him. Although he obtained some promotions in his position as a public servant, he was never suited to the law and increasingly began to pursue a musical career.

Before leaving home, he composed his earliest surviving work, a waltz

dedicated to his governess and had also started on a one act opera. During his time in St. Petersburg, he was taken to a performance of Mozart's *Don Giovanni* and was so inspired that he decided to dedicate himself to music.

At age 21, he enrolled as a pupil in the newly opened Conservatoire of Music in St. Petersburg under Anton Rubinstein and in 1865 was appointed professor of harmony at the Moscow Conservatoire under Rubinstein's brother Nicholas, after resigning his position in the public service. He composed his first symphony "Winter Dreams" (1868) and the "Romeo and Juliet Fantasy Overture" (1870). Two of his early pieces were performed by the "Waltz King" himself, Johann Strauss the Younger, at a public concert in Moscow.

Tchaikovsky managed to write two books standardising the teaching of music and earned some money as a music critic. He was constantly impoverished however, surviving by working as an accompanist and giving music lessons to a small group of students. His clothes became decidedly shabby and he was forced to move from one boarding house to another to avoid his creditors. The strain of giving lessons while still grappling with his first major orchestral works became too much for him and he found it impossible to sleep, with unremitting headaches, hallucinations and numbness in his hands and feet.

One of the main reasons Pyotr was so chronically short of money is because whenever he found himself solvent he was incredibly generous to his family and friends. It is estimated that during his lifetime, he gave away nearly half of all he earned. He was fortunate to have come under the protection of a wealthy widow, Nadezhda von Meck, with whom he communicated by letter, although incredibly they never spoke to each other.

"Only one thing is essential: that the main idea and the general outline of all the separate parts appear not by means of searching, but of their own accord, as a result of that supernatural, inscrutable and wholly inexplicable force which we call inspiration." — Tchaikovsky

With her financial help, he travelled to the south of France, from where he wrote: "I am old, and can enjoy nothing more. I live on my memories and my hopes. But what is there to hope for?" He was only 31 years old. Nadezhda continued to provide him with financial and emotional support, with the two correspondents exchanging more than a thousand lengthy and affectionate letters.

Although he risked alienating his wealthy patron, Pyotr decided to try to placate his family and attempt to rebut the looming scandal of his homosexual activities by getting married. He had received a declaration of love from a 28 year old music student, Antonina Milyukova, and after a brief courtship, they were married on 18 July 1877. Inevitably, after less than a month together, the marriage proved to be a disaster, with Pyotr finding his wife "abhorrent" and his mental state deteriorated even further as he attempted to grapple with his confused and guilty feelings. As he wrote to Nadezhda: "I longed ardently and greedily for death. Death seemed to be the only way out—but to kill myself was unthinkable."

Despite his words, he used what little money he had to drink "a good deal of wine" and waded up to his waist into the ice-strewn water of the Moscow River until his legs went numb. It was only his otherwise robust health that enabled him to avoid a fatal dose of pneumonia. He escaped to the care of his brother Anatoly, and lapsed into a coma that lasted two days. He never resumed living with Antonina, who after giving birth to a number of children with other men, was certified insane in 1896. As he wrote at the time, "Truly, there would be reason to go mad if it were not for music."

Notwithstanding all his torments during this period of his life, he was still able to produce some of his best work, composing his Fourth Symphony as well as the opera *Eugene Onegin*. He also composed one of his greatest ballets *Swan Lake,* which remains one of the most popular ballets of all time, along with his later work *Sleeping Beauty*. With Nadezhda's support, he began travelling regularly through Europe and his earlier reliance on Russian themes was gradually replaced with a more cosmopolitan approach.

His first "Piano Concerto" had been lambasted as "worthless and unplayable", but other works were gaining increasing popularity. The Andante Cantabile movement of his "String Quartet No 1 in D Major", brought the great novelist Leo Tolstoy to tears when he first heard it in 1871. When his father died, he composed the ever popular Serenade for Strings with its famous waltz movement.

Tchaikovsky described his creative process in the following terms:

> I forget everything. I behave like a madman, trembling and shaking in every limb, with scarcely enough time to jot down the sketches, so quickly do the thoughts pursue one another . . . Only one thing is essential: that the main idea and the general outline of all the separate parts appear not by means of searching, but of their own accord, as a result of that supernatural, inscrutable and wholly inexplicable force which we call inspiration.

Commissioned to write a ceremonial piece, he rattled off his famous "1812 Overture", complete with the sounds of cannons and all the din of battle, in a celebration of Russia's defeat of Napoleon's Grand Army. Tsar Alexander II was assassinated at the same time as the death of his valued tutor and mentor Nikolay Rubinstein, but Tchaikovsky continued to compose and the new Tsar, Alexander III, awarded him the Order of St. Vladimir, as well as an annuity for life.

Whenever life in Moscow became too much to bear, Tchaikovsky retreated to his sister's house at Kamenka, where he was able to compose without distraction. He was now sufficiently financially secure to look for a place of his own to rent in the country and he eventually settled into a comfortable house at Klin, about 50 miles from Moscow. He found rural life much more conducive to his creative process, as many of his melodies came to him during his strolls through the woods, although he was never free of his nervous ailments, frequently accompanied by blinding headaches.

Although by nature a solitary person, he craved companionship and an appreciative audience. He had romantic involvements with a number of young men, but remained terrified of being publicly condemned for his behaviour, concerned that it would ruin his career. He never succeeded in forming any enduring relationships (apart from the remote figure of Nadezhda).

For reasons that have never been fully explained, Nadezhda terminated both her correspondence and financial support, three years before Tchaikovsky's death. Although she was under some financial pressure, and may have concluded that her protégé's success enabled him to survive without her support, Pyotr was never able to accept her abandonment.

He overcame his nerves to conduct his own music, travelling to America, where he successfully conducted a performance of his work at the inaugural concert held in Carnegie Hall, New York. Unfortunately, he developed a painful neuralgia in his right arm, hampering his ability to continue conducting.

Tchaikovsky attended Cambridge University early in 1893, and was awarded an Honorary Doctorate of Music. He returned to Russia in time for the first performance of his last great work, the Sixth "Pathetique" Symphony, which was rapturously received. Its mournful final movement almost sounds like the harbinger of his impending death.

On 21 October 1893, Tchaikovsky took a laxative for his chronic stomach upset and later consumed a glass of unboiled water. Although rumours persist that he took his own life by consuming poison to avoid a scandal involving a young male aristocrat, the medical records of the time support the conclusion that he died after contracting cholera from the water.

He had drunk excessive quantities of vodka, cognac and wine throughout his life, as well as smoking heavily, producing a range of health issues, in addition to his precarious mental state. But the doctors who attended to him in his final days recorded that his diarrhoea had steadily worsened, accompanied by cramps, delirium and kidneys that ceased to function. Such symptoms are typical of an attack of cholera and there is simply no convincing evidence to support the hypothesis of suicide caused by poison.

Although introspective and melancholic by nature, Tchaikovsky was able to employ rhapsodic melodies and inspired orchestral effects, to compose ten operas, six symphonies, four concertos, three ballets and numerous other pieces of chamber and piano pieces as well as songs, much of which remains amongst the most popular music in the classical repertoire. Despite his unhappy and tormented life, he continued his creative work right through to the last months of his 53rd year.

As Rubinstein wrote in a letter to his sister when he heard the tragic news, "What a loss for music in Russia! And it happened in the prime of life—he was only 50!—and all this from a glass of water."

Paul Gauguin

[1848–1903]

Paul Gauguin was born in Paris in 1848, but as a result of his father's outspoken political views in opposition to the regime of Louis Napoleon, the family left France for exile in Peru, where his mother's Creole family lived. His father died during the journey. After living for a period in Lima, Gauguin served on a merchant ship and later in the French Navy, before commencing a prosperous career as a stockbroker in Paris.

Whilst working as a stockbroker, he accumulated sufficient wealth to buy paintings by Manet, Renoir, Monet, Pissarro and Cezanne, and was inspired to become a keen amateur painter himself. After meeting Pissarro, he increasingly gave his life to painting until, at age 35, he resigned his position and dedicated himself completely to his art. In 1876 he submitted a landscape to the Salon in Paris, which was accepted. He became increasingly enamoured with the style and techniques of the Impressionists, particularly Pissarro and Cezanne, who became his teachers. In 1883, he moved to Rouen with his wife and five children, so that he was able to "paint every day". He became disillusioned with the art scene in Rouen as he was unable to sell his work and he soon exhausted the modest savings he had accumulated.

His Danish wife returned to her family in Copenhagen with three of their children, and a few months later Gauguin reluctantly followed, his money depleted. His Danish paintings became noticeably "brighter, more luminous," as he described them in one of his letters to Pissarro, but the Danes were no more attracted to the new techniques than the conservative French critics. In his own words he was

> at the end of my courage and resources . . . in a foreign town without credit or money. Every day I ask myself whether I should not climb into the attic and put a cord around my neck. What prevents me from doing so is painting . . .

Gauguin returned to Paris and was sufficiently desperate to accept a job posting bills around the city. In 1886 he left to live and paint in seclusion amongst the peasants of Brittany, where he soon became the most prominent member of the Pont-Aven group of artists who tried to capture and reproduce the rugged Breton landscape and the simple faith and lifestyle of the local people. He returned to Paris at the end of the year and met the newly arrived Dutch artist Vincent van Gogh with

whom he established a close but eccentric friendship.

As an artistic movement, the Impressionists had always struggled for any enduring unity as alliances disintegrated and egos rapidly took over. After 1886, the artists essentially pursued their own objectives and methods with very few of them attaining financial success. Gauguin himself moved away from the Impressionist style as he preferred to use areas of pure, flat colour for expressive and symbolic purposes.

Gauguin stayed for a period in Martinique, but returned again to France at the end of 1887, seriously ill with dysentery and without enough money to acquire the paint and canvasses he needed to work.

He also lived for a period in Arles with Vincent van Gogh, but did not share his friend's enthusiasm for the small Provencal town. The two friends argued repeatedly and in late December 1888, the quarrel became so violent that van Gogh attacked Gauguin, causing the latter to depart abruptly and return to his group of artists in Brittany.

In April 1891 he decided to retreat even further from the increasingly industrialised world and moved to Tahiti, to depict the idyllic, primitive life of the native inhabitants, in their tapestry-like landscape. He expressed the hope that he could live there "on ecstasy, calmness and art". He describes his island life in the book *Noa Noa*:

> I have escaped everything that is artificial and conventional. Here I enter into Truth, become one with nature. After the disease of civilisation, life in this new world is a return to health.

He did not discover some untouched paradise however, and he soon became increasingly despondent, developing an addiction to morphine, which he had started to take to treat his syphilis and painful ulcers on his legs. He was shunned by the other Europeans on the island, who regarded him as an immoral and corrupting influence amongst the natives, leading him to attempt suicide in 1897.

"a sad personage named Gauguin, a famous artist, enemy of God and all that is honest" — Monsignor Martin

---

Earlier in the same year he completed what was probably his defining masterpiece "Where Do We Come From? What Are We? Where Are We Going?" in which Gauguin employs the huge canvas to represent the cycle of life, starting on the right with a sleeping girl, moving to the brightly lit figure of his "Tahitian Eve" picking fruit in the centre, and ending with an old woman approaching death. Each of the figures depicted in the painting, including the Maori god overseeing everything, has an allegorical purpose in their carefully constructed poses within the tapestry-like landscape.

Despite all his travails he continued to paint. His colourful and serene portraits of the local women going about their everyday activities in the simple environment of their villages remain some of the most evocative images of the Pacific Islands at the end of the 19th century.

Poverty and ill health compelled him to return to France for a short period, but only Degas expressed any enthusiasm for his Tahitian paintings. We now recognise Gauguin's work as powerfully original, the vivid colours depicting a state of mind rather than any attempt at capturing the reality of the scene. As Gauguin describes:

> By arrangements of lines and colours, using as pretext some subject borrowed from human life or nature, I obtain symphonies, harmonies that represent nothing absolutely real in the vulgar sense of the word; they express no idea directly but they should make one think, as music does, without the aid of ideas or images, simply by the mysterious relationships existing between our brains and such arrangements of colours and lines.

It is little wonder that his contemporaries failed to appreciate the message he was attempting to convey. He returned in frustration to Tahiti for the last time in 1895, where he remained until 1901, when he moved to the island of Dominique in the Marquesas. Impoverished, lonely and embittered, but still painting, he committed suicide on the Marquesas Islands at age 55 on 8 May 1903. His death was remarked on by the local bishop, Monsignor Martin: "Nothing of interest happened here other than the sudden death of a sad personage named Gauguin, a famous artist, enemy of God and all that is honest."

After his death, a retrospective exhibition of his best work was held at the Salon d'Automne in Paris, belatedly earning him the reputation and influence on later artists, which he continues to enjoy to this day.

There are two reasons why Gauguin has earned his place in our *Whatever it Takes* list of struggling artists. Firstly, he had enjoyed a comfortable life as a prosperous stockbroker and even though he knew his decision to abandon it would cost him dearly, he remained determined to pursue his artistic inspiration to some of the most remote areas of the world. Secondly, he had a loving relationship with his wife and five children. We cannot ignore how much they also must have suffered from Gauguin's life choices, particularly when two of his children were seriously ill while still quite young. Nevertheless, he was so committed to his artistic inspiration that he was prepared to sacrifice that part of his life, abandoning his family in his lonely pursuit of artistic perfection.

Vincent van Gogh

[1853–90]

Born in Holland during the height of the Impressionist Movement, van Gogh ultimately rejected its techniques as too constrained, failing to give the artist enough freedom to express his emotions. He was the first outstanding Dutch painter for nearly 200 years, but as he did not take up painting until ten years before his death, he left himself only limited opportunities to make his mark. Although his dedication and output during these years took on an almost frenzied nature, he remained virtually unappreciated during his lifetime.

His father had been a Methodist pastor, and although his mother was a competent artist and three of his uncles were art dealers, all attempts to encourage him in a career selling art were miserable failures. After working for the Goupil art dealership in The Hague, he was sent to London where he became obsessed with the landlady's daughter, Ursula Loyer, in what was the first of many disastrous attempts to find happiness with a woman. He also began to display pronounced mood swings and what we would now describe as symptoms of a bipolar disorder.

He then worked for a period in Paris, before effectively being dismissed. He had begun to embrace a form of religious fanaticism, resulting in him spending time as a lay preacher amongst the impoverished coalminers of Borinage in Belgium. Imbued with humanitarian zeal, he gave away all his worldly possessions, but was soon dismissed from his position as a result of his too literal interpretation of Christ's teaching.

He remained in Holland between 1881 and 1885, during which time he increasingly devoted himself to painting as his new "mission" in life with "his pencil becoming more and more obedient every day".

After embarking on a disastrous relationship with a pregnant prostitute, Sien, he contracted gonorrhoea and had to be hospitalised for weeks to undergo zinc sulfate injections, but there was no cure nor escape from the condemnation of his pious parents. He rarely bathed and smelt of turpentine and tobacco from the pipe that was almost continuously clenched between his few remaining teeth.

As one of his biographers wrote:

Plagued by loneliness, Vincent never ceased to yearn for closeness with another human being . . . To be united with a woman in love was the most pressing desire of Vincent's adult life even though his desire was doomed to frustration. Although he craved companionship, he praised his own alienation as a necessary part of his creative life.

After leaving Siena, he reconciled with his parents after returning to live with them in 1884, and began painting street scenes, people and landscapes. Despite being attracted to the colours used by the Impressionists, his palette remained dominated by sombre browns and greys. After the sudden death of his father in 1885, he drew on his earlier experiences working with the poor to produce his first major painting, "The Potato Eaters", which depicted a profound sympathy for the plight of the underprivileged, using thick, dark daubs of paint. He wrote in a letter to his brother Theo on 30 April 1885:

> I have tried to emphasise that those people, eating their potatoes in the lamplight, have dug the earth with those very hands they put in the dish . . . I have wanted to give the impression of a way of life quite different from that of us civilised people. Therefore I am not at all anxious for everyone to like it or admire it at once . . .

Unfortunately for Vincent, this prediction characterised the rest of his life, as although Theo worked in the large Goupil & Cie Gallery in Paris where he devoted his working life to promoting the new art of the Impressionists, his brother's art failed to attract interest. During the course of their adult lives, Vincent sent his brother 658 letters, all of which have survived, and in return Theo sent him money, usually as much as a third of what he earned, enabling the chronically impoverished artist to buy paint, canvasses, tobacco and sometimes even food when he bothered to eat.

Vincent returned to Paris in the spring of 1886, arriving on his brother's doorstep unannounced. In that same year, Gauguin had decided to leave the city to paint in the isolation of Brittany, although the two met when Gauguin returned, and soon developed a close friendship.

With his brother's encouragement, Vincent began to absorb some of the Impressionist's colourful techniques, using lighter colours with shorter brushstrokes. Although at times he appreciated and even admired their work, he was initially disappointed in the paintings his brother displayed of leading French artists at the time. He describes his first reaction to the art of the Impressionists: "ugly, sloppily and badly painted, badly drawn, of a poor colour; everything that is miserable."

He found it difficult to get on with his fellow artists and decided to remain true to his own vision of art: "I am too absolutely and utterly convinced that I am, after all, on the right path when I paint what I feel and feel what I paint—to worry too much about what people say of me." And later: "The worse I get on with people, the more I learn to have faith in nature and concentrate on her."

In February 1888, he retreated to Provence in southern France, where he remained for the last two years of his life. Here he produced some of his greatest masterpieces, utilising what we now recognise as a vibrancy of colour and bold brushstrokes that no other artist ever matched. He was particularly stimulated by the scenery around Arles and decided to "use colour more arbitrarily, so as to express myself forcibly," emphasising that he was now trying to "exaggerate the essential and to leave the obvious vague".

In "Wheat Field and Cypress Trees" (1889), van Gogh filled one of his most famous landscapes with ecstatic movement, with both the vegetation and the sky filled with overpowering turbulence. Even the hills and the clouds heave with the same undulant motion. In his letters to his brother he provided eloquent descriptions of his choices in colour and the emotional meanings he attached to them. Yellow for example meant faith or love, while carmine was a spiritual colour, cobalt a divine one; red and green on the other hand represented terrible human passions.

Van Gogh worked frantically, as if to make up for all the years he missed before he started painting, and in little over a year produced 200 paintings and 100 drawings.

Gauguin arrived to stay with him in October 1888, and despite their contrasting approach to art and fiery tempers, they worked together for a period; but they constantly fought and the more they drank, the more they quarrelled. In December 1888, his increasingly fractious friendship with Gauguin culminated in van Gogh attempting to attack Gauguin, resulting in Gauguin abruptly departing for Paris. Van Gogh became sufficiently distraught to cut off the lobe of his ear, which he bizarrely presented to his favourite prostitute Rachel before being admitted to hospital.

Although Theo had just announced his engagement to the great love of his life, he rushed south to be with his brother, finding him in an agitated and delusional state, barely coherent. Vincent's doctor, Dr Rey describes how van Gogh insisted on lying down in someone else's bed and refused to leave before finally getting up to try and wash himself in the coal-box. He was committed to an asylum, but appears to have recovered quickly and was discharged on 7 January 1889.

Vincent returned to his painting, including his favourite sunflowers and a number of anguished self-portraits, including some depicting his still-bandaged ear. After acquiring a taste for absinthe from Gauguin, Vincent became even more delusional, suffering auditory and visual hallucinations, leading him to admit himself into the Asylum of St. Remy on 8 May 1889, where he remained for the better part of a year.

Vincent was given a separate room as a studio and, between repeated seizures and spells of madness, was able to resume painting, although he "continually hears shouts and terrible howls of the animals in a menagerie".

Only his loving and loyal brother fully understood what Vincent tried to portray in his art and the terrible toll that the artist had to endure to produce it. Theo alone recognised that his brother had "captured the sun, given a blessing to the world, a benediction of colour". As Theo perceptively wrote to his fiancée: "One first has to relinquish all one's conventional ideas in order to grasp what he means. But one day he will be understood."

After sending a consignment of his latest paintings to his brother, Vincent suffered another breakdown and attempted to poison himself by eating the paint off his brushes. While back in the asylum he received news that the only painting he was ever able to sell, "The Red Vineyard", had been purchased by a fellow artist Anna Boch, at an Art Show in Brussels.

"Which is the madder—a man who would cut off his own ear, or a man who would pay $80 million for one of his paintings?" — Paul Cox

---

Despite further relapses from which he never fully recovered, van Gogh somehow completed more than 200 canvasses in a 15 month period. Almost all of the pieces that are now so prized were produced in the last two years of his life, when he was battling for his own survival and attempting to preserve his sanity.

Looking at his brutally frank self-portraits from this period, we can see how his inner torments were beginning to dominate his life. "I am risking my life in my work and half my reason is gone," he wrote, also describing himself as a green shoot springing from the roots of an old felled tree: "The more I am spent, ill, a broken pitcher, by so much more am I an artist—a creative artist."

Although he remained close to his brother Theo, they both suffered from an enduring melancholia. Theo was later committed to an asylum and his sister Wilhelmina also suffered from a chronic psychotic illness, causing her to spend nearly 40 years in an asylum. Their younger brother Cornelius committed suicide.

As well as battling his manic-depressive condition, van Gogh suffered from epilepsy, schizophrenia, poisoning from absinthe abuse, porphyria and probably Ménière's disease.

With the help of Pissarro, and in order to be closer to his brother Theo, van Gogh was accommodated in the home of Dr Gachet at Auvers-sur-Oise, just 20 miles north of Paris. Although it took a while for the two men to relax in each other's company, Vincent eventually found the kindly doctor a comfort to him and he completed a number of portraits of him, with the same red hair and fair skin as himself. He continued to paint at a frantic pace, completing a further 70 canvasses in the last 70 days of his life; but van Gogh found life increasingly unbearable. His abject poverty continued and he suffered recurrent nervous crises with hallucinations and depression.

In an urgent letter dated 27 July 1890, delivered to Theo in Paris, Dr Gachet advised that Vincent had "wounded himself", and Theo rushed once again to his brother's side. The police accepted that Vincent had accidentally shot himself, and although his death was painfully slow, he finally died in his brother's arms on 29 July 1890.

With his art unappreciated and no cure for his mental illness in sight, it is equally possible and widely accepted that van Gogh committed suicide when only 37 years old. The nature of his suicide was unbelievably distressing—having shot himself in a wheat field near Auvers, it took him two days to die of his injuries. Theo wrote to his mother, "He has found the rest he so much longed for."

I cannot leave van Gogh's life without recounting the story of his memorable portrait of the kind hearted Dr Gachet, which broke all records when it was sold at the Christie's New York art auction on 15 May 1990 to a Japanese art dealer for $82.5 million. The buyer's identity was disclosed the following day as Ryoei Saito, a Japanese billionaire paper manufacturer.

The astonishment of the art world soon turned to outrage however, when the eccentric Mr Saito announced that, upon his death, he had instructed that the painting should be placed in his coffin to be cremated with him, so that his heirs could avoid paying Japan's crippling death duties.

Fortunately for all lovers of art, Saito's Daishowa group got into financial difficulties and Saito himself was arrested for bribing a provincial governor, resulting in the collapse of his empire. One of his banks seized the van Gogh painting, along with Renoir's *Au Moulin de la Galette*, saving the paintings. Saito died in April 1996 and was cremated with his wishes unfulfilled.

As Australian movie director Paul Cox pointed out when making his film *Vincent*, "Which is the madder—a man who would cut off his own ear, or a man who would pay $80 million for one of his paintings?"

Of all the cruel and tragic ironies of van Gogh's life, surely the greatest is that after living in extreme poverty as a result of selling only one of his more than 900 paintings, a portrait of the doctor who helped care for him in his final days should later be sold for a price that made it at the time the most expensive painting ever sold.

Henri de Toulouse-Lautrec

[1864–1901]

Although from a wealthy aristocratic French family, Henri de Toulouse-Lautrec was the product of parents who were first cousins and, as a result of an inherited illness, he was frequently weak and often sick. He was born at Albi on 24 November 1864, but after breaking both legs as a young boy, he never grew beyond the height of a dwarf; his head was abnormally large and he walked with difficulty, rendering him acutely aware of his physical limitations. His childhood miseries were not helped by his father, who made no secret of the fact that he was repelled by his son's physical deformities.

After moving to Paris as a 19 year old he began drinking heavily, and embarked on a career as an artist to console himself for being unable to pursue an active life. After obtaining early art lessons from Rene Princeteau, a well-known painter of sporting subjects, he worked mainly on sporting images until he was 24. He then enrolled in the studio of Leon Bonnat and later Fernand Cormon and became the interpreter par excellence of Parisian night life, having set up his own studio in Montmartre in 1885.

He felt a strong empathy for the dissipated and sometimes grotesque life of those he painted and became well known in the bars and nightclubs he frequented for his sketches of the people he encountered, which he transferred to canvas or print with bright colours and simple lines. He led a dissolute life in the seedy areas of Paris and painted in startling reality the scenes he inhabited in the nightspots and brothels of Montmartre, before dying of alcoholism and venereal disease aged only 36.

Initially he painted mostly sporting subjects, but soon began to concentrate on the characters of the bars and nightclubs in Montmartre where he lived. Lautrec was a great admirer of Degas and on one memorable occasion, after a particularly riotous evening, he took a group of friends to the modest flat of Mademoiselle Dihau in Montmartre, as dawn was approaching. She admitted them in their evening attire with some hesitation, but was mollified by the sight of Lautrec guiding his friends to the paintings of Degas and ordering them to kneel in reverence before the work of a master.

Lautrec himself was without peer as a graphic artist and his posters, which combined the words of the venue with a design representing the

essence of the establishment, have probably never been matched. In his lithographs, he adopted Japanese modes of print design with superlative effect. He was also a gifted portrait artist, and his depiction of Vincent van Gogh in pastel and Oscar Wilde in watercolour are masterful images of his subjects.

His simplified technique conveyed a profound hatred of any pretence, and like his own character his work displayed an endearing, warm-hearted approach, full of sympathy tinged with despair. Despite the unhappiness of his own life, he never allowed his circumstances to corrupt the authenticity of his art. The young Picasso was one of many artists in Paris influenced by Lautrec's work.

He was paid an allowance by his parents and also earned some money from the sale of his art, but he was always short of money, despite a surprisingly prodigious output, because of his extreme extravagance.

He met Gauguin in 1888 and some of Gauguin's flat, rhythmic patterning of colour can be recognised in Lautrec's *"Au Cirque Fernando".* From 1890, he became an almost permanent fixture at the Moulin Rouge and his first picture of its interior, *"Au Moulin Rouge: La Danse; Dressage des nouvelles"* was proudly displayed in the cabaret's entrance foyer. He also became an habitué of Paris' *maison closes,* producing numerous paintings and drawings of the working girls in sympathetic tones.

Among the many subjects he portrayed were the cabaret singer and

"his stocky arms had massive hands with club-like fingers . . . He had very large nostrils, bulbous lips, a thickened tongue and a speech impediment. He sniffed continuously and drooled at the mouth." —Julia Frey

actress Yvette Guilbert and the dancer *La Gouloue* ("The Glutton"), who invented the can-can. She can be seen adjusting her bright orange coiffure in the background of his painting "At the Moulin Rouge". In the same painting we can recognise a portrait of the diminutive artist, seated next to an unusually tall man. *La Gouloue* is also featured in his first and most famous poster completed in 1891, showing her performing her famous dance on stage at the Moulin Rouge.

In 1895 Lautrec travelled to London, where he produced his portrait of Oscar Wilde, but an exhibition of his paintings in London in 1898 was not a success. After returning to Paris in the same year, his dissipated lifestyle and advanced syphilis necessitated treatment in a sanatorium, where he continued to produce his famous *"Au Cirque"* drawings by relying on his memory. He died at the Chateau de Malrome, Gironde on 9 September 1901.

"He had a normal torso," writes biographer Julia Frey, "but his knock-kneed legs were comically short and his stocky arms had massive hands with club-like fingers. His bones were fragile and would break without apparent cause. He limped and had very large nostrils, bulbous lips, a thickened tongue and a speech impediment. He sniffed continuously and drooled at the mouth." Despite physical handicaps and debilitating conditions, Lautrec raised himself above his predicament to enjoy a consistently productive life depicting the murkier aspects of life in Montmartre.

Unlike van Gogh, he did find a limited market for his work during his lifetime, but, like many of his debauched contemporaries, Lautrec's short life was blighted by alcohol and syphilis. He left as his legacy a unique collection of pictures and graphic drawings of the prostitutes, barmaids, dancers and singers who inhabited his dissolute world.

There are more than 600 of his works still exhibited in the museum named after him in his native city of Albi. Included in the display is Lautrec's cleverly modified walking stick, which had been specially hollowed out to include a small glass and flask of brandy so that the great artist was never without a drink.

Virginia Woolf

[1882–1941]

Adeline Virginia Stephen was born into a wealthy upper class family on 25 January 1882. Both her parents had literary interests, but hers was not a happy childhood, particularly as she lived amongst eight children from different relationships and was sexually abused as a young girl. Her mental health was not only severely compromised by this abuse, but by a family background of mental and psychological disorders. Her sister Stella was repeatedly raped by a demented cousin, James Stephen, who, before being eventually placed in an institution, was widely believed to have been the notorious "Jack the Ripper".

Although far saner than many writers, Virginia believed that her moments of insanity were vital to her creative functioning. As she wrote to a friend in June 1930, after experiencing a severe bout of "fertile illness",

> As an experience, madness is terrific I can assure you, and not to be sniffed at; and in its lava I still find most of the things I write about. It shoots out of one everything shaped, final, not in mere driblets, as sanity does.

She felt "exquisitely happy" in the presence of hallucinations and delusions, which served to intensify her senses. But later in her troubled life, the process had reversed and her creative mania had been transformed into a black depression, living at the precarious edge of "a great lake of melancholy" which caused her to doubt whether she would ever write again.

Woolf believed that there was a kind of nobility, a truth in her pain, which, although it caused her to suffer terribly, was a level of anguish that enabled her to create great fiction. She knew she was unstable, but realised these waves of disturbance allowed her to access levels of her own inventiveness that would not otherwise be possible. Among the most creative female writers, she faced almost unimaginable obstacles and challenges just surviving, let alone succeeding despite her gender.

She almost died of whooping cough when six years old and whilst still recovering her strength, was sexually assaulted by her 19 year old step-brother Gerald, who molested her on the pantry shelf. Because she could see the reflection of her experience in a mirror, she could never again look at herself in a mirror without reliving the trauma of what

occurred. It may have also led to the eating disorders from which she suffered throughout her life. Gerald's sexual exploitation of Virginia and her sister Vanessa continued throughout their childhood and Virginia found comfort in the arms of her accommodating sister.

Despite her experiences in such a dysfunctional family, Virginia grew up to be outwardly a witty and confident young lady whose company everyone enjoyed. However she did appear at times vulnerable, unpredictable and certainly eccentric, and her manic episodes and psychotic hallucinations were so pervasive that it is amazing she was able to cope at all, let alone produce such a volume of memorable writing.

She coped by absorbing herself in reading and writing about her experiences, originally in her diaries, and later in her books, using fictional characters like "Miss Jan" to express her innermost fears and play out all the unresolved dramas in her troubled life. Although she later spent many months of her life totally incapacitated by her condition, she would live in her imagination and ultimately emerge from the experience to use her mental torment as a fertile source for her writing.

Both Virginia and her father had been profoundly affected by the death of her mother, who died of influenza when Virginia was 13. She locked herself in her room, refusing to eat, with the unfortunate elder sister Stella not only assuming the role as head of the household, but also being called upon to become her father's lover in place of his deceased wife. Stella only escaped by marrying in 1897, but her life ended when she returned from her honeymoon and contracted appendicitis, which was so incompetently treated by doctors that she died soon afterwards, leaving 15 year old Virginia with the loss of her mother substitute as well. Vanessa was then called upon to assume the role of her father's lover and accompanied him to many society functions.

In 1904 her father died of bowel cancer, followed shortly afterwards by the death of her most beloved brother, Thoby, from typhoid fever, reducing Virginia to such an agitated state that it required three nurses to keep her under control. Her persistent episodes of mental illness deteriorated into a complete breakdown, causing her to be briefly institutionalised.

Two years later, Vanessa also married, causing Virginia to feel so betrayed by her sister that she seduced her husband to exact her revenge. Virginia was now 30 and had begun to establish her literary career. On meeting Leonard Woolf, a Jewish student who had attended Cambridge on a scholarship, she decided he would be a safe and reliable companion, although she made it clear to him that he would never be allowed to have sex with her even though he was totally besotted with her. They shared a passion for literature and he reluctantly assumed the role of the comforting companion who would reassure her when she was wracked with doubts about her work, even though she never permitted the marriage to be consummated.

On completing her final draft of *The Voyage Out* she experienced her worst breakdown, becoming completely paranoid and babbling almost incoherently for days on end as she stopped eating and could not sleep at all without the aid of pills. Like later episodes, she emerged from the experience with her creative inspiration reinvigorated, causing her to controversially conclude that madness was her muse. *The Voyage Out* was published as her first novel in 1915.

In an attempt to assist his wife, Leonard brought home a small hand-operated printing press and together they started Hogarth Press. This enabled both of them to print and disseminate their own work, and Hogarth Press eventually became one of the most highly regarded publishing houses of the day. It published not only the works of its owners, but also writers like T.S. Eliot, Laurens van der Post, Katherine Mansfield and a number of foreign writers. Having started its life as a distracting form of therapy for Virginia however, Hogarth Press soon became so successful that it became a drain on her energy and time.

> *"Her innocence had been stolen from her. All she had learned to do was hide inside herself."* — Octavia Wilberforce

Although she repelled the advances of her husband, Virginia craved affection and began a torrid affair with an aristocratic artist, Vita Sackville-West, which lasted for the next 15 years, even though both women remained ostensibly married to their respective husbands. Virginia took an overdose of barbiturates after returning from visiting Vita, but it was probably precipitated by an argument with Leonard, who had understandably become jealous of his female rival.

Although her father had originally convinced her that reading and writing were deleterious to her nervous condition, with Vita's help, Virginia began to vary her reading and writing routines, and by avoiding activities that sapped her energies she was better able to manage her condition.

She was a great admirer of the American writer Henry David Thoreau and praised his statement: "The millions are awake enough for physical labour, but only one in hundreds of millions is awake enough to a poetic or divine life. To be awake is to be alive."

She wrote *Orlando* in 1928, dedicating it to her beloved Vita, tracing the journey of its androgynous protagonist through an extraordinary four centuries. Vita's son Nigel described it as "The longest and most charming love letter in literature."

A later biographical work *Flush* (1933), revolves around the life of Elizabeth Barrett Browning's pet spaniel and provides a dog's-eye view of the love affair between his mistress and the poet Robert Browning.

Despite her incurable problems and conflicts at home, by the end of

1931 Virginia had produced a number of her classic novels, including *Mrs Dalloway*, *To the Lighthouse*, *Orlando* and her best and most personal work to date, *The Waves*, as well as an impressive body of poetry and literary criticism. She had attained celebrity status, and began involving herself in promoting the cause of women, embodied in her 1938 book *Three Guineas*, which explored the plight of women and their oppression.

When Hitler invaded Europe and threatened Britain itself, her matrimonial home, including the offices of Hogarth Press, were destroyed in the blitz. Leonard and Virginia became so concerned that they stockpiled lethal doses of morphine to prepare for a suicide pact. Leonard was increasingly succumbing to his own depression, causing further resentment from his wife because of how closely he monitored her. Her pacifist views also meant that she opposed her husband's decision to join the Home Guard.

Her final diary entries in March 1941 show her life and reason unravelling, as she was still haunted by her childhood. She consulted her friend and physician Octavia Wilberforce, who recorded

> even after all these years, she felt burdened with grief for her father, and yet was also terribly resentful. She had not been allowed to have a proper childhood. Her innocence had been stolen from her. All she had learned to do was hide inside herself. This might be an excellent tool for a writer, but it was hardly adaptive for someone struggling to stay in contact with the world.

In a letter to her sister Vanessa, she wrote: "I feel I have gone too far this time to come back again. It is just as it was the first time, I am always hearing voices, and I know I shan't get over it now." After praising Leonard for all he had done for her she concluded by saying, "I can hardly think clearly any more . . . I have fought against it, but I can't any longer."

Although some feminist writers have attempted to blame Leonard for her suicide, the last words she wrote render such a conclusion highly unlikely. In her last note of endearment for Leonard she wrote:

> What I want to say is that I owe all the happiness of my life to you. You have been entirely patient with me and incredibly good . . . If anybody could have saved me it would have been you.

She walked out of their house and filled her pockets with heavy stones, before wading into the nearby River Ouse, where she was carried to her death downstream. Her body was not recovered for three more weeks, and poor Leonard never recovered—although he did not die until he was 88 years old, he remained celibate for the rest of his life, even after remarrying.

Ernest Hemingway

[1899–1961]

It is cruel to start the story of a man as vitally masculine as Ernest Hemingway by describing his ending, but we need to understand his circumstances in order to explain why a brilliantly successful writer, who had always taken life head on, would choose to end it with a shotgun at age 61.

Hemingway lived in Cuba from 1946 until 1960, when he retired to the small town of Ketchum in the Boulder Mountains of Idaho, close to the ski resort of Sun Valley. By July of 1961, his previously robust body was gaunt and emaciated, as he was acutely depressed and suffering from hypertension. He was also suffering from paranoid delusions and hallucinations and was unable to sleep. He had found himself impotent and lost his memory as a result of the electroconvulsive therapy he received for his hypertension and depression.

Although his fourth wife had been sufficiently concerned about his mental state to put a padlock on the gun safe, Hemingway had found the key, selected his favourite shotgun and placed it in his mouth, before pulling the trigger and blowing his head off. Hemingway's father had done the same thing with the same revolver that his own father had used in an unsuccessful attempt to take his life after suffering painful wounds in the Civil War.

Hemingway had been awarded both the Pulitzer Prize and a Nobel Prize for literature, as the author of classics such as *The Sun Also Rises*, *For Whom the Bell Tolls* and *The Old Man and the Sea.* When he received the Nobel Prize in 1954, *Time* magazine described him as "a globe-trotting expert on bullfights, booze, women, wars, big game hunting, deep sea fishing and courage".

In his most recent biography, written for the first time by a woman, Hemingway's "code" is described as: "A tough, stoic approach to life that seemingly substitutes physical courage and ideals of strength and skill for other forms of accomplishment." Although she predictably describes it as "tiresomely macho", her appraisal is nevertheless accurate except in relation to his writing skills.

Hemingway was born on 21 July 1899 in the suburbs of Chicago, the second eldest of six children, with a deeply religious father who abhorred alcohol and gambling. His father was a successful physician, committed

to the outdoors and physical fitness, imparting to his son a love of fishing and hunting, resulting in young Ernest being able to shoot well and catch his own fish before he was even three. However his father constantly battled depression, sometimes to the point of paranoia and being completely dysfunctional.

His mother Grace dominated the household and introduced Ernest to music and literature. She had an excellent singing voice and helped to support the growing family by composing songs as well as giving music lessons, although Hemingway insisted that her spending habits were always extravagant. She avoided domestic chores and left most of the cooking to the family cook and her husband. She also insisted that her son be dressed in pink frocks and flowered bonnets at least until he was six years old. His mother treated her two elder children as twins, cutting their hair and making them dress in identical clothes. It is little wonder that although they were close as children, Hemingway was to later develop a violent hatred of his elder sister that was never resolved.

His mother tried in vain for many years to persuade him to play the cello, but Ernest was more interested in boxing and outdoor activity. Her attempts to encourage his appreciation of literature were much more fruitful however, and with the help of a teacher, Fannie Briggs, Hemingway submitted his first short story at the end of junior year. He was soon contributing regular articles to a local newspaper, particularly on sporting subjects; although one of his school publications was so derogatory of the staff that he was nearly expelled.

After finishing school, his family helped him to take a position as a cub reporter for the *Kansas City Star*, where he learnt the skill of being able to write quickly in short sentences of "vigorous English" with precision and clarity. His time in Kansas also saw him begin his lifelong attachment to heavy drinking and he supposedly fell in love for the first time with an actress called Mae Marsh. Although the match seems improbable, given their age difference and the fact that she was a highly paid star, Hemingway had grown into a dramatically physical man with swaggering good looks.

America entered World War I on 6 April 1917 and Hemingway was keen to take part. He signed up with an infantry regiment, but soon realised that his bad eyesight would prevent him being accepted into the army. A friend who had lost his eye in a golfing accident had worked as an ambulance driver with the Red Cross in France, and the two men signed up for service in Italy where the war against the Austrians was producing heavy casualties. Before leaving New York he had purchased an expensive engagement ring for Mae, but we hear nothing more about her, apart from her marriage to another man later in the year.

Hemingway was never happier than in the company of men in a shared adventure and he seemed to have approached his war experience as something comparable. He was particularly impressed by the fact that lower ranks were required to salute the Red Cross volunteers as they were to be treated as officers. He served on the Italian front, where he was seriously wounded on 8 July by an exploding Austrian mortar shell, near Fossalta. One of his companions was killed by the explosion and another had both his legs blown off. He later remarked that you "have to hurt like hell before you can write seriously". Like most of his life experiences, allowing for some embellishment, his wartime exploits inspired his later writing when he published *A Farewell To Arms*.

When he was later challenged for attempting to glorify the circumstances of his injuries, he stated: "It is not unnatural that the best writers are liars. A major part of their trade is to lie or invent and they will lie when they are drunk, or to themselves, or to strangers." In fairness to Hemingway, he was decorated for his bravery in rescuing another badly wounded man, despite his own wounds and being hit by machine gun bullets in the process. Whatever the truth of the matter, he carried pieces of shrapnel and scars with him for the rest of his life and the episode brought him to prominence for the first time, waving a crutch at the cameraman from his wheelchair in a newsreel.

The war changed him in other ways—he became much more ego-centric, irascible and always craving attention and adulation. He also carried the emotional scars of being rejected by the beautiful nurse who helped him through his rehabilitation. As James Nagel wrote, Agnes von Kurowsky's rejection "hurt him severely, so deeply that he wrote about it all his life".

After returning from the War, he began giving lectures on his experience, even producing his blood-stained and shredded trousers to an astonished audience. He worked for a period in Toronto, but soon realised that his talents as a writer were being stifled by the demands of editors and advertisers.

In October 1920, he met and fell for Hadley Richardson, a woman seven years older than him, and they married the following year. Apart from their physical attraction, they both shared a desperate desire to escape their families, particularly in Hemingway's case from his increasingly domineering mother. Inspired by the stories told by Sherwood Anderson, they moved to Paris for seven years to be part of the growing literary scene in the city, joining writers like Henry James, T.S. Eliot, F. Scott Fitzgerald, Ezra Pound and James Joyce.

Although Pound was almost the only reader who found merit in the poems Hemingway wrote, he persisted in the genre, and had some limited success having some of them published. He came under the influence of Gertrude Stein, who gave him valuable advice as a writer, although they eventually had a bitter falling out when Hemingway overheard her making disparaging remarks about him to her lesbian lover Alice B. Toklas.

In his autobiography, *A Moveable Feast*, Hemingway recounted his "early days" in Paris as "very poor and very happy". He wrote that he was a quiet, but quick-tempered and impatient youth, who emerged as someone troubled and surprisingly insecure despite his outgoing nature. He describes his life as "uncompromising, punishing the fine and the foul impartially, taking its own grim time, choosing its own grim methods".

Partly because of his childhood experiences, Hemingway became obsessed with hair and insisted on his wife cutting her hair short to expose the back of her neck while he grew his long, like some of the Japanese painters he had met. He visited Spain regularly and became extremely knowledgeable about every aspect of bull fighting, which he later displayed in his writing, particularly in *Death in the Afternoon*.

After being appointed foreign correspondent for the *Toronto Star Weekly*, he decided to use his position to live the life of a world adventurer that could feed his burgeoning skills as a writer. Fancying himself a boxer, he regularly picked fights with anyone who offended him or his honour. He also ridiculed his fellow writers, including Sherwood Anderson and Sinclair Lewis and fought lifelong feuds with former close friends like John Dos Passos, and later even Stein and Fitzgerald.

Apart from writing, alcohol seemed to be his primary obsession and he also found some success betting on the horses. Although he described many happy times with Hadley, their marriage began to sour in part because of his belief that sexual orgasms diminished his creativity. His attitude reminds me of the great line from French novelist, Honoré de Balzac on sex—"There goes another novel." He could also never forgive his wife for misplacing a suitcase crammed with almost everything he had written (including the carbon copies).

Nevertheless they returned to Toronto for the birth of their son John, after which they went back to Paris as Hemingway had resigned from his job as a journalist. Despite the distraction of fatherhood, Hemingway wrote some of his best stories during this time and began to attract a wider audience than the Paris set. He was impressively good looking and so full of energy and enthusiasm that people gravitated to him as the centre of attention, but there were early signs of manic behaviour beginning to emerge and some bouts of severe depression.

His first published book of stories, *In Our Time*, came out in 1925 and the author was soon completing his first novel *The Sun Also Rises* (published in October 1926 to great acclaim), based on his time in Pamplona for the famous Festival of San Fermin. He also wrote a dreadful attempt at satire in *Torrents of Spring*. It was typical of Hemingway to mercilessly lampoon two characters in his first two books, unmistakably Harold Loeb and Sherwood Anderson, both of whom had been instrumental in promoting Hemingway when he was an unknown author.

Pauline Pfeiffer was a wealthy writer for *Paris Vogue* and had become one of Hadley's friends, but she and Ernest could not resist each other and although he probably did love both of them in his own selfish way, he ultimately abandoned Hadley for her former friend and she and Ernest married in May 1927 after he had converted to her Catholic faith.

On returning to America, they discovered the allure of Florida Keys, where Hemingway developed his lifelong passion for deep sea fishing with his "Mob" of male friends. It was at this time that his father Ed took his life with the same pistol used by his own father in what had been a failed suicide attempt, and Hemingway was wracked with guilt for not having done more for his father.

He continued to write despite ongoing battles with depression, especially after receiving news of his father's suicide in December 1928. He was furious at his father's cowardly act and after asking his mother to send him the revolver, he threw it into a nearby lake (perhaps just so that he would not be tempted to follow the example of both his father and grandfather).

Although he was a prolific writer, he found it an exhausting process requiring him to rework every paragraph until he was satisfied with it. "The most essential gift for a good writer is a built-in, shock-proof, shit detector," is a well known quote of his.

Although his fame as a successful writer was assured, his tantrums and violent outbursts of temper only increased, with his bouts of depression becoming more prolonged and more crippling. Throughout his life he was obsessed with death, with five of his seven major novels ending in a tragic death—even his first story, published when he was still at high school, ends in suicide. He had a hair fetish (although he began to lose his own hair) and compulsively counted everything from the fish and birds he killed, to the number of words he had written each day. He displayed so many dysfunctional symptoms that later psychoanalysts have had a field day with diagnoses ranging from narcissism, personality disorder, post-traumatic stress disorder as well as latent homosexuality.

He was always aggressive and reckless and had numerous accidents, including one where he pulled a skylight onto his forehead leaving him visibly scarred for the rest of his life. Other accidents involved motor vehicles, planes and hunting. On one occasion, he shot himself in the leg trying to dispose of a hooked shark alongside his boat. Although he remained in contact with his family, he was ruthless in his treatment of his siblings, with only his sister Ursula escaping his wrath, principally because she lived in Hawaii.

Despite regular hunting safaris to Africa, Hemingway was bored with his life. When his new love interest, Martha Gellhorn, encouraged him to help with the war against the Fascists in Spain, he joined the conflict. Although his Loyalists ultimately lost the war, he drew creative inspiration from the tragedy and was inspired to write one of his greatest novels, *For Whom The Bell Tolls*, based on this period.

His marriage to Pauline ended and he moved to Cuba with Martha, but unlike his previous wives, Martha was not prepared to accept his domineering behaviour and heavy drinking—in company with the roughest elements on the island—and they fought constantly. His biographer Jeffrey Meyers was undoubtedly correct in observing that, like many other creative spirits, Hemingway "found liquor an instant relief from the oppressive strain of writing as well as an anodyne for the even greater torments of creative sterility".

Although his fourth wife had been sufficiently concerned about his mental state to put a padlock on the gun safe, Hemingway found the key.

His popularity derived also from his collections of short stories, which many critics regard as the genre best suited to his writing style. From his first collection *In Our Time* (1925) through to *The Fifth Column and the First Forty-Nine Stories*, Hemingway maintained an economical and focussed intensity in his writing that appealed to a wide readership.

Incredibly, Hemingway spent much of World War II running an officially sanctioned spy network against the Germans in Cuba, and even equipped his fishing boat as a sub-hunter. But the conflicts with Martha became only more violent and he belatedly decided to travel to the battlefields of Europe, where he managed to witness part of the D-Day invasions some distance off shore. Before leaving London he had another serious car accident, with his head striking the windscreen, causing some brain damage, although he was too eager to see action to have it properly treated.

Although he was travelling as a war correspondent with the army, he managed to have himself issued with a weapon and did kill a number of Germans in different conflicts. He even deliberately exposed himself to enemy fire on more than one occasion. With the usual difficulty separating fact from fiction, it does appear that he assisted the Free French forces to liberate Paris and he undoubtedly took it upon himself to personally "liberate" the plush Ritz Hotel, where he found suitable accommodation for himself and his entourage.

True to form, he had by then embarked upon a new relationship with Mary Welsh, who soon became his fourth wife. His writing responded to the excitement of new stimuli and although his new wife was fully aware of his capacity for emotional and physical abuse, she remained loyal and supportive. On one memorable occasion, he took two Luger revolvers, given to him by a friendly American general, and used them to obliterate a photo of her last husband in the toilet of their suite in the Ritz, causing extensive flooding in the hotel.

Hemingway's attitude to women was the same as his approach to hunting—it was all about stalking the prey and capturing her or, in the case of an animal, killing it. Once the trophy had been achieved, you could boast about it; you could put her in a story; you could put the horns on the wall, or parade her beauty in front of your admirers, but any enduring interest in an ongoing relationship was never his priority. She was only there to be enjoyed until the next target loomed in his sights, and then he was off again in pursuit of a new challenge. The conquest was the thing, not the commitment.

Despite his obvious flaws, his fame only increased when he returned to Cuba as a war hero and "Papa" Hemingway now attracted the rich and famous to the island, including Jean-Paul Sartre and the actors Gary Cooper, Marlene Dietrich, Ingrid Bergman and Ava Gardner. Although his life was beset by suicides and premature deaths during 1951, he continued writing, completing his masterpiece *The Old Man and the Sea*, which describes his time in Cuba. It was widely praised and earned him a Pulitzer Prize.

As well as losing his publisher Charles Scribner, and Pauline, the mother of two of his children, his relationship with his sons Patrick and Gregory deteriorated. The former succumbed to mental illness and the latter developed drug problems, mental instability and, worst of all for his father, overt transsexualism, appearing in public dressed as a woman.

Returning to Africa to reclaim his reputation as the "great white hunter", he was devastated when he realised that his infirmity had ruined his hunting skills, leading (incredibly) to him being appointed a Game Warden. He was involved in two plane crashes, the second of which resulted in a fractured skull, dislocated shoulder, ruptured spleen and kidney, compressed vertebrae and loss of vision and hearing.

Hemingway took great delight in reading his own obituaries after it was widely reported that he had died in the crash. Although warned that his continued drinking would have fatal consequences, he could not survive without alcohol and he had further cause for celebration when he was awarded the Nobel Prize for Literature in 1954.

Castro's seizure of power as well as Hemingway's ongoing health issues, prompted him and Mary to return to America, where they settled in the idyllic mountain scenery of Idaho. Here he completed his autobiography, *A Moveable Feast*, after a trunk full of his notebooks dating from his time in Paris between the wars was unearthed in the basement of the Ritz. Shortly prior to his suicide, he wrote in the Foreword: "This book contains material from the remises of my memory and of my heart. Even if the one has been tampered with and the other does not exist."

His overall health and mental instability continued to worsen and by the end of 1960 he was told by his doctors that, in addition to his almost unrelenting pain, he had developed a form of diabetes that would render him blind and impotent within the next few years.

His paranoia about being followed and having his phone bugged assumed real proportions when the Director of the FBI, J. Edgar Hoover, arranged to have his activities monitored. Admitted to the Mayo Clinic, supposedly for treatment of his hypertension, the doctors decided that he would benefit from Electroconvulsive Shock Treatment, which after a dozen treatments left him even more paranoid, delusional and depressed. Worst of all it completely obliterated his memory. He was administered a further ten sessions, leaving him a drooling idiot, who had lost 75 pounds, with no possibility of him ever resuming his life as a writer.

Little wonder that shortly after he returned home, he found his shotgun and took his own life, just as his father had done, and his brother Leicester, his sister Ursula, and his granddaughter Margaux. His sons also suffered lifelong psychological abnormalities.

Charles Bukowski

[1920–94]

In 1986, eight years before his death, the poet and writer Charles Bukowski was described by *Time* magazine as "the laureate of American low-life". Although he had written hundreds of short stories, thousands of poems and over 60 books, including six novels, he had never achieved a wide readership in America outside his base in Los Angeles, but in Europe he had an enormous following. Over 2.2 million books had been sold in Germany alone, where he was born.

His father had served in the American Armed Forces in Germany after World War I and after marrying a local girl, their son Heinrich (later to call himself Charles), was born barely six weeks later on 16 August 1920, in Andernach. The family moved to America when Heinrich was two years old and eventually settled in Los Angeles, where his father struggled to support his family during the Depression.

Bukowski survived a traumatic childhood of frequent beatings from his father and cruel tormenting from other children because of his German accent, dyslexia and severe acne, which produced enormous pustules on his face and back, requiring frequent draining of pus and blood by needle, leaving him significantly scarred for the rest of his life.

In a 2003 film of his life, "Bukowski: Born Into This", he stated that his father beat him with a razor strap for five years until he was 11. He said that the experience helped his later writing because it enabled him to understand undeserved pain. After a final confrontation with his abusive father, in which young Bukowski knocked his father out cold, he left home to live on the streets, surviving on occasional menial jobs. He travelled across America and lived for a while in New York, but after his first attempts at writing short stories and essays were all rejected by a number of publishers, he abandoned writing and became what he described as "a ten year drunk", a regular troublemaker at bars all over the country.

On 22 July 1944, he was arrested for suspected draft evasion and was imprisoned for 16 days before being discharged as unfit for military service as a result of failing a psychological examination. He was arrested at least three more times for drunkenness. "I don't like jail—they got the wrong kind of bars in there," he wrote.

Returning to Los Angeles, he treated his local bar as a hiding place,

arriving at 5am for free drinks before the place opened at 7am, staying there until closing time, before going home to catch a few hours sleep and repeating the cycle the next day.

In 1955, he suffered a near-fatal bleeding ulcer, causing his doctors to warn him that if he resumed drinking he would be dead in months. Although he completely ignored this advice for the next 38 years, his brush with death inspired him to start writing poetry. Drawing on his experiences of living rough on the streets, he began to chronicle the plight of the desperate and the down-and-out, in vivid and moving terms in his poems and stories. His language was brutal but honest and he began to develop a following on the West Coast, after some of his writing was published in fringe and porn magazines. His early success was based on the simple formula "write a good story and throw in some goddam sex."

Incredibly, he was able to hold down a job for two periods of his life, delivering mail and working in a post office. Although he hated it, he was beginning to write frequently, including a regular column called "Notes of a Dirty Old Man", in a local underground paper *Open City*. His approach to the column was no more complicated than: "Just sit by the window, lift the beer and let it come."

At age 49, he decided to dedicate himself to writing, saying: "I have one of two choices—stay in the post office and go crazy . . . or stay out here and play at writer and starve. I have decided to starve." Fuelled by scotch and beer, Bukowski managed to complete his first novel *Post Office* in 1969 over a period of 19 nights after quitting his job. He never gave up drinking but spent more time drinking and writing at home. As he described his writing: "I like to drink and write and have the novel happen to me and I'm as surprised as anyone else."

Niall Griffiths describes Bukowski's novels in an Introduction to a later edition of *Post Office* as "messy, ramshackle, rambling and structurally chaotic," thrusting his writing into the world as he did himself—"beer-bellied, flatulent, crude, aggressive, sensitive, acne-scarred, everything".

Bukowski described himself as not a nice man who liked "desperate men, men with broken teeth, and broken minds and broken ways. They interest me. They are full of surprises and explosions. I also like vile women, drunk cursing bitches with loose stockings and sloppy mascara faces."

Despite his scarred appearance, bulbous red nose, dodgy teeth and pot belly, women inexplicably found Bukowski attractive even before he developed a cult following. Among his many relationships, the most enduring was with Janet Cooney Baker, who was one of the few who could match his alcohol consumption, before she drank herself to death in 1962. In 1964, he had a daughter with his de facto Frances Smith and later he had a short lived marriage to Barbara Frye, the publisher of *Poetry* magazine, followed by a tortured and tumultuous affair with Linda King, a poet and sculptor. Most of his relationships were with hookers, some of whom gouged out pieces of his flesh with their fingernails, when he was too drunk to defend himself. Far from being embarrassed by his appearance, he flouted it, declaring, "I have this mug that sells books."

Not surprisingly, he had numerous health issues, and attempted suicide multiple times. As he described himself: "I have some trouble with the stomach, my liver gets overloaded and my haemorrhoids are threatening to take over the world, but what the hell. I'll make it."

Bukowski wrote the screenplay for the 1987 movie *Barfly*, starring Mickey Rourke playing Bukowski, and Faye Dunaway as a composite of some of his women, but Bukowski was not impressed with the way his character was portrayed.

In September 1987, he was interviewed at length by Sean Penn, who was to play his character in another movie loosely based on his life. Penn described Bukowski as "a notorious boozer, brawler and womanizer". Bukowski told Penn: "I do all my creative work when I'm intoxicated," and that after going through a four year period in his life without sleeping with a woman, "Writing is more important than any woman."

> *"I also like vile women, drunk cursing bitches with loose stockings and sloppy mascara faces."* — Bukowski

Like his hero Ernest Hemingway, Bukowski always drank heavily and was obsessed with betting on horse races, with only mixed success: "When you have a suicide complex, nothing bothers you . . . except losing at the track." He admitted to Penn that he was a fan of the valet at the local racetrack, who taught him "The worse it gets, the wiser I get." After his death, Penn dedicated his movie *The Crossing Guard* (1995) to Bukowski.

Bukowski describes his approach to writing in his poetry:

> Unless it comes out of
> Your soul like a rocket,
> Unless being still would
> Drive you to madness or
> Suicide or murder,
> Don't do it.
> Unless the sun inside you is
> Burning your gut,
> Don't do it
> When it is truly time,
> And if you have been chosen,
> It will do it by
> Itself and it will keep on doing it
> Until you die or it dies in you
> There is no other way
> And there never was.

"It's simple, it's either you get it down on paper or you jump off a bridge."

His epitaph, "Don't Try", reads somewhat enigmatically, but its meaning was revealed in a letter he wrote to John Corrington in 1963, where he explained his creative approach: "You don't try. That's very important: not to try, either for Cadillacs, creation or immortality. You wait and if nothing happens, you wait some more. It's like a bug high on the wall . . . You wait for it to come to you. When it gets close enough, you reach out, slap it and kill it or if you like its looks you make a pet out of it."

Although he had made his reputation rubbishing middle class values, the royalties from his stories eventually enabled him to settle into San Pedro suburbia, complete with pool, hot tub and black BMW, where he spent his last years with his wife Linda Lee Beighle.

Although the amount of alcohol he consumed each day would have killed most people at a young age (as his doctors had predicted), he lived into his eighth decade and ultimately died of cancer. Rather than being handicapped by the grog, his writing seemed to thrive on it. Unlike many of his contemporary "beat" generation writers, Bukowski did not do drugs; but alcohol was the yeast that made his writing rise above the mundane, permitting even his frequent profanities to flavour the stories he told so well.

He was a writer whose language reflected not only his personality, but all the sordid details of his life. He wrote from the gutter about the low-lifes, whores and drunks who inhabited it with him, using their language and syntax, with an honesty that won admirers all over the world. He was the ultimate survivor, overcoming all that life threw at him, to record his experiences in a volume of writing that in 2006 was donated by his widow to the Huntington Library in San Marino California.

He died of leukaemia at 73 on 9 March 1994, after having spent most of his life in what one critic described as "a certain taboo male fantasy, the uninhibited bachelor, slobby, anti-social and utterly free".

Conclusion

THE ONE THING WE CAN CONFIDENTLY CONCLUDE from all the individuals we have examined is that to succeed at anything you need a clear vision of what you are trying to achieve and a determination to attain it. Most of us are not leaders, nor are we outstanding artists, but in our own modest ways, we all have ambitions and dreams we would like to see fulfilled. It is my fervent hope that the lives I have summarised will inspire readers of all abilities to accept that we can all achieve our potential if, believing in ourselves, we have the confidence to overcome, or at least ignore, the obstacles and objections we will encounter along the way.

Life will present hurdles we cannot surmount, but we should resolve to address the issues we can control, to lead life in accordance with what we believe, without being unduly distracted or censored by those who don't agree with us.

All of the people we have studied achieved something worthwhile or memorable. Yet, despite the spectacular achievements of many in the first group, those of the second group have bequeathed to us the more enduring legacy, because true art has a timeless appeal, which despite changing fashions, will always find a place in our hearts.

In politics and on the battlefield, success usually depends upon the effective and sometimes ruthless wielding of power. By contrast, in artistic endeavours, personal success is more often incidental to what matters, as artists struggle with internal challenges that can be debilitating, to find a way to express their originality and creativity. What both have in common is the *Whatever it Takes* characteristic that is the theme of this book—the capacity to overcome whatever stands in the way to achieve what they see as their destiny.

What can we conclude from the lives of the tragic artists? Some were probably born crazy, or at least were always going to have their crazy moments which in some way seem to have helped them to create the inspired legacy they left. Others were driven mad by demons they had to grapple with all their troubled lives, so that their art was despite their madness, rather than a result of it. There were others like Beethoven, Schubert and Gauguin, who were only able to overcome their suicidal tendencies because creative inspiration gave them sufficient reason to live.

For some like van Gogh and Woolf, there is evidence to support their belief that their perceived madness played a direct role in their creative output. Despite the criticism of such an idea by some psychiatrists, who are we to dispute or criticise the insight that the artists themselves have described? Perhaps Seneca was right more than 2,000 years ago when he wrote "There is no great genius without the touch of some madness."

We also know from the lives of Schumann and Hemingway that they were so debilitated during periods of acute depression that they were quite incapable of dealing with reality, let alone having the energy and will to focus on their art. Perhaps we should conclude that it is only the milder forms of mental disorders that can have any productive effect. Artists suffering from the worst of mental distress are completely incapable of organising and recording their thoughts in any intelligible order. In the depths of their disorder, their condition is simply too incapacitating for them to be productive.

But when they emerge from the depths, they are able to "rely on their imagination to build bridges between their inner and external world," as Michael Fitzgerald puts it. In other words, these artists connect the world of their creative imagination with the real world, by erecting their artistic bridges and finding an artistic expression for the sensations they have experienced.

The same idea is contained in Kay Jamison's book, in which she describes many instances where artistic work is inspired by the manic state and may even be executed whilst still under its sway, to be edited or refined once the artist is able to emerge from the worst of the condition to something closer to normal. The process she describes could be compared to the story told by Samuel Taylor Coleridge in producing his poetry, of the amazing visions and ideas inspired by his drug-induced condition, which he attempted to recall and record in poetry once he emerged from the effects of the drugs.

Others suffered from physical ailments as well. Most of our 19th century artists were victims of syphilis, which was essentially incurable until the later invention of Penicillin. The victims of the disease found it increasingly debilitating and wholly destructive of any potential relationships—whether it was a cause or part of the effect of their overall mental state.

Edgar Allan Poe, who is hardly read today, may have been correct when he wrote that "much that is glorious and all that is profound" may be the product of "that loftiest intelligence" that inspires the troubled artist, even though many people would call it a madness.

Would they have been as productive and original without their afflictions? We will never know of course, but it cannot be doubted that part of what made them so impressive as artists operating in their chosen fields, was the very problems that caused them so much distress and misery. They all in their way succeeded in overcoming their problems sufficiently to produce an enduring legacy, even though they paid a terrible price for the pleasure they have continued to afford us.

The tragic unhappiness of most of the lives we have examined exemplifies what Alex de Jonge wrote about Baudelaire in the passage quoted earlier, where he referred to the artist who tries to capture the spirit of his own disaster and can only do so by "stretching his nerves beyond breaking point and building his art from the pieces of a shattered self".

Lines from a poem by Stephen Spender make a fitting final tribute to the outstanding individuals whose lives we have examined, particularly the artists:

> The names of those who in their lives fought for life,
> Who wore at their hearts the fire's centre
> Born of the sun, they travelled a short while toward it
> And left the vivid air signed with their honour.

Further Reading

Part 1

Brooks, David. "When the Good Do Bad", *New York Times*, 19 March 2012
Green, John Richard. *A Short History of the English Speaking People*, 1992
Hollis, James. "Why Good People Do Bad Things", PhD thesis, 2008
Machiavelli, Niccolo. *The Prince*, 1513 (translated by Allan Gilbert)
McFarlane, K.B. *Lancastrian Kings and Lollard Knights*, Oxford 1972
Plutarch. *Parallel Lives*, "Alexander", "Julius Caesar", "Pompey", "Themistocles"
Rummel, R.J. *Death by Government*, 1994
Veznikova, Ivana. "The Lucifer Effect: Understanding How Good People Turn Evil", *Vienna Review*, 1 November 2006
Zimbardo, Philip. *The Lucifer Effect*, 2007

NICCOLO MACHIAVELLI
Celenza, Christopher S. *Machiavelli: a Portrait*, Harvard University Press, 2015
Machiavelli, Niccolo. *Discourse upon the First Ten Books of Livy*, 1517 (translated by Allan Gilbert, 1965)
Unger, Miles J. *Machiavelli: a Biography*, Simon and Schuster, 2011
White, Michael. *Machiavelli: a Man Misunderstood*, Little, Brown, 2004

JULIUS CAESAR
Dennison, M. (derived from Suetonius). *The Twelve Caesars*, 2012
Gelzer, M. *Caesar, Politician and Statesman*, 1968
Holland, Tom. *Rubicon: the Triumph and Tragedy of the Roman Republic*, 2003
Kamm, Antony. *Julius Caesar: a Life*, Routledge, 2001
Shakespeare, William. *Julius Caesar*, 1559, Act 3, Scene 2
Suetonius. *The Lives of the Caesars*
Yenne, Bill. *Julius Caesar: Lessons in Leadership from the Great Conqueror*, Palgrave Macmillan, 2012

EMPEROR JUSTINIAN I
Browning, R. *Justinian and Theodora*, 1971
Herrin, Judith. *Byzantium: The Surprising Life of a Mediaeval Empire*, 2007
O'Donnell, James J. *The Ruin of the Roman Empire*, 2009
Procopius, *The Secret History*, 550 (translated by G.A. Williamson and Peter Sarris, Penguin, 2007)
Rosen, William. *Justinian's Flea: Plague, Empire and the Birth of Europe*, 2006

EMPEROR CHARLEMAGNE
Anonymous Saxon poet. *The Life of Charles the Great*, written in 890
Barra, Geoffrey. *The Crucible of the Middle Ages*, 1999
Moss, H. St. L. B. *The Birth of the Middle Ages*, 1935, Chapter XIV
The Royal Frankish Annals, written in late 9th and early 10th centuries
Wickham, Chris. *Medieval Europe*, 2016
Williams, Hywel. *Emperor of the West: Charlemagne and the Carolingian Empire*, Quercus, 2010

POPE INNOCENT III
Costen, Michael. *The Cathars and the Albigensian Crusade*, 1997
Jacob, E.F. "Innocent III", in J.B. Bury ed. *Cambridge Mediaeval History*
Linder, Douglas. *A Brief History of Witchcraft Persecutions before Salem*, 2005
Smith, Charles Edward. *Innocent III: Church Defender*, 1951
Tillman, H. *Papst Innocenz III*, 1954

KING HENRY V
Curry, Anne. *Henry V: Playboy Prince to Warrior King*, Allen Lane 2015
Curry, A. *The Battle of Agincourt: Sources and Interpretations*, Boydell Press, 2009
Hibbert, Christopher. *A Brief History of the Battle of Agincourt*, 2000
Maxwell-Lyte, H.C. *Historical Notes on the Use of the Great Seal of England*, 1926
Vale, Malcolm. *Henry V: The Conscience of the King*, Yale University Press, 2016
Wavrin, Jehan de. *Chronicles and Ancient Histories of Great Britain, 1399–1422*, (translated by Sir William Hardy and Edward Hardy. 1887)

SIR THOMAS MORE
Ackroyd, Peter. *The Life of Thomas More*, 1991
Bacon, Francis. *Apophthegms New and Old*, 1625
Marius, Richard. *Thomas More*, 1984
Marshall, Peter. *Heretics and Believers: A History of the English Reformation*, Yale University Press 2017
More, Thomas. *A Dialogue Concerning Heresies*, 1530
More, Thomas. *Correspondence of Sir Thomas More*, E.F. Rogers ed., 1947
More, Thomas. *Utopia*, 1516
Wilson, Derek. *England in the Age of Thomas More*, Hart-Davis, 1978

TSAR PETER THE GREAT
Anderson, M.S. *Peter the Great*, 1978
Kliuchevskii, V. *Peter the Great*, 1965
Massie, Robert K. *Peter the Great: his Life and World*, 1980

OLIVER CROMWELL
Abbott, William Cortez. *The Writings and Speeches of Oliver Cromwell*, Clarendon Press, 1939
Churchill, Winston. *A History of the English-Speaking People*, abridged edition 1998
Miller, Leo. *John Milton and the Oldenburg Safeguard*, 1985
Morrill, John. *Oliver Cromwell and the English Revolution*, 1990
Richards, Peter. *For Life, Liberty and Property*, 2003
Robertson, Geoffrey. *The Tyrannicide Brief*, Chatto and Windus, 2005
Scott, David. *Politics and War in the Three Stuart Kingdoms 1637–1649*, Palgrave Macmillan, 2004

NAPOLEON BONAPARTE
Fauvelet de Bourrienne, Louis Antoine. *Memoirs de Napoleon Bonaparte*, 1855
Hochschild, K.F.L. *Desiree: Queen of Sweden and Norway*, 1890
Holland, Rose J. *The Censorship under Napoleon I*, 1918
Horne, Alistair. *The Age of Napoleon*, 2006
Lefebvre, George. *Napoleon*, 2009, Book 1
Ribbe, Claude. *Le Crime de Napoleon*, 2005
Ries, Ferdinand. *Biographical Notes on Ludwig van Beethoven*, 1838

ADMIRAL HORATIO NELSON
Lavery, Brian. *Horatio Lord Nelson*, London 2003
Nelson, Horatio. *Autobiography of Lord Horatio Nelson*, 1799
Nelson, Horatio. "Sketch of my Life", biography provided to John M'Arthur
Southey, Robert. *Life of Nelson*, 1813
Sugden, John. *Nelson: the Sword of Albion*, 2012

THEMISTOCLES
Frost, Frank J. *Plutarch's Themistocles: A Historical Commentary*, 1980
Holland, Tom. *Persian Fire*, 2005
Lenardon, Robert J. *The Saga of Themistocles*, 1978

THE SALEM WITCH TRIALS
Brooks, Rebecca Beatrice. *History of the Salem Witch Trials*, 2011
Dane, Anthony, and Nancy Schultz. *Salem: Place, Myth and Memory*, Northeastern University Press, 2004
Lawson, Deodat. *A Brief and True Narrative of Some Remarkable Passages Relating to Sundry Persons Afflicted by Witchcraft at Salem Village*, 1692

Mather, Cotton. *Memorable Providences, Relating to Witchcrafts and Possessions*, 1689
Proctor, John. *Petition*, Salem Prison, 23 July 1692
Schiff, Stacey. *Annals of Terror: the Witches of Salem. Diabolical Doings in a Puritan Village*, 2015
Schiff, Stacey. *The Witches Salem 1692: a History*, Weidenfeld and Nicolson, 2015

ABRAHAM LINCOLN
Donald, David Herbert. *Lincoln*, 1995
Keneally, Thomas. *Abraham Lincoln*, Lipper/Viking 2003
Levy, George. *To Die in Chicago: Confederate Prisoners at Camp Douglas, 1862–1865*, 1994
Morris, Jan. *Lincoln: A Foreigner's Quest*, 1999
White, Ronald C., Jnr. *A. Lincoln: a Biography*, 2009

RANAVALONA, QUEEN OF MADAGASCAR
Pfeiffer, Ida. *The Last Travels of Ida Pfeiffer: Inclusive of a Visit to Madagascar* (translated by H.W. Dulcken, 1861), Palala Press edition, 2016.

AUNG SAN SUU KYI
Ibrahim, Azeem. *The Rohingyas: Inside Myanmar's Hidden Genocide*, Hurst and Co., 2016
Popham, Peter. *The Lady and the Generals: Aung San Suu Kyi and Burma's Struggle for Freedom*, Rider Books 2016
Popham, Peter. *The Lady and the Peacock*, 2011

Part Two

Chilvers, Ian. *The Oxford Dictionary of Art*, 3rd Edition
Drabble, Margaret, ed. *The Oxford Companion to English Literature*, 6th Edition, 2000
Fromm, Erich. *The Heart of Man*, 1964
Jamison, Kay Redfield. *Touched with Fire*, 1993
Janson, H.W., and Anthony Janson. *History of Art*, 5th Edition, 1997
Jeremy, Nicholas. *The Great Composers*, 2007
Jones, Jonathan. *The Lost Battles*, 2012
Kottler, Jeffrey A. *Divine Madness: Ten Stories of Creative Struggle*, 2006
Milton, John. *Paradise Lost*, 1667
Moore, Thomas. *The Works of Lord Byron*, Vol. 13, p. 24
Ousby, Ian, ed. *The Cambridge Guide to Literature in English*, 1992
Rewald, John. *The History of Impressionism*, 4th Edition
Scholes, Percy A. *The Oxford Companion to Music*, 10th Edition
Vasari, Giorgio. *The Lives of the Artists*, 1568 (translated by George Bull, 1957)
Zara, Christopher. *Tortured Artists*, 2012

THE ALTAMIRA CAVE PAINTINGS
Bahn, Paul G. *Cave Art: a Guide to the Decorated Ice Age Caves of Europe*, Frances Lincoln, 2012
Bahn, Paul G. *Prehistoric Art*, 1998
Breuil, H. and H. Obermaier. *The Cave of Altamira at Santillana del Mar, Spain*, Tipoagrafia de Archivos, 1935
Cueva de Altamira. *Museo de Altamira*, Cantabria
David, Bruno *Cave Art*, Thames and Hudson, 2017

MICHELANGELO
Gayford, Martin. *Michelangelo: his Epic Life*, Fig Tree, 2013
Brion, Marcel. *The Medici: a Great Florentine Family*, 1969
Goldshieder, L. *Michelangelo: Paintings, Sculpture, Architecture*, 1953

JOHN MILTON
Barasch, Mosche. *Blindness: the History of Mental Image in Western Thought*, 2001
Beer, Anna. *John Milton: Poet, Pamphleteer and Patriot*, 2008
Milton, John. *The Doctrine and Discipline of Divorce*, 1643
Milton, John. *Areopagitica*, 1643
Milton, John. *Tenure of Kings and Magistrates*, 1649

LUDWIG VAN BEETHOVEN
Barry, Cooper. *Beethoven*, Oxford University Press, 2008
Beethoven, Ludwig van. Letter to Karl Amenda 1 July 1801
Beethoven, Ludwig van. Letter to Franz Gerhard Wegeler 29 June 1801
Lockwood, Lewis. *Beethoven: the Music and the Life*, 2005 edition
Robbins Landon, H.C. *Beethoven: a Documentary Study*, 1974
Swafford, Jan. *Beethoven: Anguish and Triumph: a Biography*, Faber and Faber 2014

FRANZ SCHUBERT
Gibbs, Christopher Howard. *The Life of Schubert*, Cambridge University Press, 2000
Ho, Desiree. "Franz Schubert's Illness: the Melancholy of an Autumnal Sunset", *Interlude*, 7 October 2011
Newbould, Brian. *Schubert: the Music and the Man*, University of California Press 1999

ROBERT SCHUMANN
Ostwald, Peter F. *Robert Schumann: Music and Madness*, Gollancz, 1985
Taylor, Ronald. *Robert Schumann: his Life and Work*, Universe Books, 1982

CHARLES BAUDELAIRE
Baudelaire, Charles. *Etudes et Temoignages*, C. Pichois, 1967
Baudelaire, Charles. *Oeuvres Completes*, 1963 Edition
Jonge, Alex de. *Baudelaire: Prince of Clouds*, 1938
Leakey, F.W. *Baudelaire and Nature*, 1968
Sartre, Jean-Paul. *Baudelaire* (translated by Martin Turnell, New Directions, 1967)

PYOTR TCHAIKOVSKY
Blakesley, Rosalind P., and Tatiana Karpova. *Russia and the Arts*, 2016
Warrack, John. *Tchaikovsky*, 1973
Weinstock, H. *Tchaikovsky*, 1943
Wiley, Roland John. *Tchaikovsky*, 2009

PAUL GAUGUIN
Osborne, Harold. *The Oxford Companion to Art*, 1970

VINCENT VAN GOGH
Bakker, Nienke, Louis Van Tilborgh, and Laura Prins. *On the Verge of Insanity: Van Gogh and his Illness*, Mercatorfonds, 2016
Heiligman, Deborah. *Vincent and Theo, the Van Gogh Brothers*, 2017
Van Gogh, Vincent. *The Complete Letters of Vincent van Gogh*, New York Graphic Society, 1958

HENRI DE TOULOUSE-LAUTREC
Felbinger, Udo. *Henri de Toulouse-Lautrec: Life and Work*, Konemann, 1999
Frey, Julia. *Toulouse-Lautrec: a Life*, 1994

VIRGINIA WOOLF
Bell, Quentin. *Virginia Woolf: a Biography*, 1996
Casamagno, Thomas C. *The Flight of the Mind: Virginia Woolf's Art and Manic-Depressive Illness*, 1996
Nadel, Ira. *Virginia Woolf*, Reaktion, 2016

ERNEST HEMINGWAY
Dearborn, Mary V. *Ernest Hemingway: a Biography*, Knopf, 2017

CHARLES BUKOWSKI
Bukowski, Charles. *Betting on the Muse: Poems and Stories*, Black Sparrow, 1996
Bukowski, Charles. Interview with Glenn Esterly, *Rolling Stone*, 17 June 1976
Bukowski, Charles. *On Writing*, Abel Debritto ed. Canongate, 2016
Cherkowski, Neeli. *Bukowski: a Life*, 1991
Dougherty, Jay. *Introduction to Charles Bukowski*, 2007
Fox, Hugh. *Charles Bukowski: a Critical and Bibliographical Study*, 1969
Sherman, Jory. *Bukowski: Friendship, Fame and Bestial Myth*, 1981
Sounes, Howard. *Charles Bukowski: Locked in the Arms of a Crazy Life*, 1998